Short

Dinners at Home

How to Order Cook and Serve Them

Short

Dinners at Home
How to Order Cook and Serve Them

ISBN/EAN: 9783744792158

Printed in Europe, USA, Canada, Australia, Japan

Cover: Foto ©Andreas Hilbeck / pixelio.de

More available books at **www.hansebooks.com**

DINNERS AT HOME

HOW

TO ORDER COOK AND SERVE THEM

By SHORT

"Come HOME to men's business and bosoms."—*Bacon.*
"A dinner lubricates business."—*Boswell.*
"Appetite comes with eating."—*Rabelais.*
"The vulgar boil, the learned roast an egg."—*Pope.*
"Nay, there may yet some monstrous region be
 Unknown to cook."—*Shakespeare.*
"Some pigeons, Davy,
A couple of short-legged hens, a joint of mutton, and
Any pretty little tiny kickshaws; tell cook."—*Shakespeare.*

LONDON
KERBY & ENDEAN 190 OXFORD STREET
1878

PREFACE.

—o—

A POPULAR idea exists that only those who can afford to give high salaries to their cooks can expect good dinners served at their own tables, and, as a consequence, many gentlemen are driven to dine at their Clubs rather than incur the risk of having both their temper and digestion spoiled by the incompetency of their cooks.

It must be acknowledged that at the present day most ladies of moderate incomes do not pay sufficient attention to their CUISINE. A mistress of a house should know how to order a dinner, how the various dishes are dressed, so as to be able to explain them to her cook, and she should see that there is a sufficiency of every necessary ingredient, without which it is impossible for a cook to do justice to her menu.

"Dinners at Home" is specially designed to give the Mistress of the Household such information as will enable her, without her constant attendance in the kitchen, (as is erroneously supposed essential by many), with a cook of moderate pretensions, to have a THOROUGHLY SATISFACTORY DINNER SERVED AT HOME.

The order in which the receipts are placed will, it is hoped, be a considerable help, both to the mistress and servant. The cook who will profit by them is not the professed artiste—nor on the other hand, one who knows nothing of the elements of cookery. I suppose her to be active—with taste for her work, and desirous of improving herself. If she be willing to follow these receipts exactly as they are written I will undertake to say that, in a short time, she will have added considerably to her knowledge, and be a "*wiser and a better*" cook.

SHORT, 1877.

CONTENTS.

	PAGE
Hints for the Mistress of the House,	9-12
Hints for the Cook,	13-17
Menus,	18-23
Soups (Potages),	25-47
Fish (with Sauces),	49-69
Entrees,	71-109
Vegetables,	111-124
Releves (Removes),	125-138
Rots (Roasts),	139-146
Savoury Dishes,	147-164
Entremets (Sweets),	165-197

HINTS FOR THE MISTRESS OF THE HOUSE.

BE very careful about having the meat well kept, according to the season of the year. Either order or choose it yourself at the butcher's. You cannot expect, if the cook have to go out marketing every morning, that she can prepare the servants' dinner and the lunch as they ought to be done, and send up the late dinner properly dressed. Let everything be at her hand.

Lay out in your mind a bill of fare for each day in the week, and order the meat required accordingly.

Keep your own stores, and give out what is wanted for each day.

Write your orders for the cook daily, with separate orders for the greengrocer, fishmonger, &c., as they call. Your presence in the kitchen should not now be required till next morning.

A visit once a-week to the butcher's is quite sufficient, as a general rule. One special object of this little work is to guard against large joints, which are in reality more extravagant than the smaller and more tempting made-dishes.

It is a mistake to have these "for company" only; for then the cook, accustomed to serve up nothing but joints, gets confused, and lamentable results follow; whereas, if she have daily training in small dishes, as a matter of course all goes well when a few friends join the home circle.

It is a good plan to have one made dish every day in the family dinner, and to practise it till perfect—then begin with another, and so on till you have a list of tested dishes, which you can always vary to the size and pretensions of your party.

Get the butcher to give you five or six pieces of neck of mutton every week, such as he calls the "*fair end*," for cutlets. Always have them ready for an emergency.

Loin chops are considered best; but for cutlets I prefer the part I have mentioned. The scrag attached to the neck is good for mutton broth, but unless you want it for that purpose, it is better to pay a little more per pound for the neck without it.

I do not approve, as some do, of dividing a leg of mutton. If you wish to make more than one dish out of it, I prefer half boiling it, then cut off as many steaks as you require, dust them with pepper and salt, broil over a clear fire, and serve *very hot* with gravy. The remainder of the leg can be made into a hash of mince, curry, or rissoles, and will be all the better for the meat having been half-cooked.

To be succulent and tender the steaks must be cut off the leg while hot, otherwise they will be hard and unpalatable.

As to a fillet of beef, some butchers will cut it for you out of the sirloin, and charge you in proportion; but where this is not the case the only way to use the sirloin after the fillet is cut out is to stew it, for if roasted it will be found to be dry and hard. A very nice small round of beef is procured by buying from twelve to fourteen pounds of ribs of beef. The butcher will take out the bones (a valuable addition to the stock pot), and roll it. If too large it can be cut in two, and it will give you two good roasts (a skewer must be run through to keep it in shape). One can be put into pickle and makes an excellent miniature round of beef.

Never allow inferior butter to be used in cooking. I have known many a dish upon which the cook had probably spent much time and trouble utterly spoiled by rancid butter.

In addition to the articles generally found in every kitchen, the following are also necessary or the receipts given in this book :—

The American whisk.
Sausage machine (for rissoles, sandwiches, &c.).
Digester (for making soup to hold ten quarts).
One dozen Timbale cases (for little puddings, Timbales of maccaroni, &c.).
Two soufflé dishes (for fondus, soufflés, &c.).
Scoop (for cutting out the core of apples).
A Flat tin baking dish.
A tin saucepan, into which fits a china saucepan, on the principle of the French *Bain-marie*, water being put in the outer saucepan, by which means the dish is steamed instead of boiled.
Two medium-sized copper saucepans, with lids to hold fire.

HINTS FOR THE COOK.

WELL wipe the meat every day, pepper it, and be very careful to cut out the kernel in the fat, which extends to the meat and gives it a taint. By not paying proper attention to this the meat has often an unpleasant taste.

Be sure the saucepans are always well cleaned before they are put away, and try and keep one for the use of each dish you are in the habit of cooking.

Weigh out every ingredient in each receipt, —some cooks will not do this, but trusting to the rule of thumb, utterly fail.

Dripping is far better for frying fish than either lard or butter, and a careful cook will always have plenty at hand. The following is an excellent way of clarifying dripping. Put it into a basin, pour over it some boiling water, and stir it round with a silver spoon; set it to cool, and then remove the dripping from the sediment, and put it into jars. Keep in a cool place.

The cook ought to know how to *sauter*. This means to dress anything quickly in a small pan with a very little butter, oil, or lard—whereas frying means boiling in hot fat.

GRAVY.

Never be in the house without stock or gravy. If you have to buy meat for it, get neck of beef, cut in dice, and fried a nice brown. One quart of water to each pound of beef, boiled down to half. Peppercorns, a little thyme and parsley added. Let the gravy boil slowly until rich enough, then strain, and when cool remove the fat. Let it boil up, season if necessary, and thicken with a teaspoonful of corn-flour, mixed smooth in cold water, to about half a pint of gravy.

ROAST MEAT OR FOWL.

The old-fashioned roaster is supposed to be the best for roasting meat, but as the close range is now almost always used instead of the open one, the following directions will be found useful :—

Grease the pan with fat before the meat is put into the oven. Then pour over the meat 2 or 3 tablespoonsful of water, and while roasting keep turning and basting continually; and you will find when it is done you will have a quantity of rich gravy, which strain through a strainer, and serve with the meat in a sauce boat. The great secret is to have the oven hot, and never to close the door completely. There must be free ventilation, or the condensed heat will cause the meat to have an unpleasant flavour.

COOKING CHOPS AND STEAKS.

They should be cooked over a clear red fire, on which the gridiron should be placed two minutes before the meat is laid on it.

LARDING.

Every cook ought to know how to lard. Poultry and white game are much improved by it, and several entrées have to be larded; and by following the excellent receipt of Soyer, it ought to be done easily:—"Lay your meat lengthwise, upon a clean napkin, across your hand, forming a kind of bridge with your thumb at the part you are about to commence at, then with the point of the larding needle make 3 distinct lines across, $\frac{1}{2}$ inch apart, run the needle into the 3rd line at the further side of the meat, and bringing it out at the first, placing one of the larded pieces in it (these ought to be about 2 inches in length, and rather more than $\frac{1}{8}$th of an inch in width), draw the needle through, leaving out $\frac{1}{4}$ inch of the bacon at each line; proceed thus to the end of the row, then make another line half-an-inch distant, stick in another row of larded pieces, bringing them out at the second line, leaving the ends of the bacon out all the same length, make the next row again at the same distance, bringing the ends out between the larded pieces of the first row, proceeding in this manner until the whole surface is larded in chequered rows."

When larding poultry, dip for one moment into boiling water in order to make the flesh firm.

TO PREPARE BACON FOR LARDING.

It is much better to prepare your own bacon for larding, as what is bought is often rancid and unwholesome.

Get a piece of bacon the thickness of two fingers, and weighing from 3 to 5 lbs. (thin bacon is the best), put it into an earthen dish, spread some ground salt at the bottom and over the bacon. Add a glass of cold water; and turn the bacon from time to time in the pickle. A fortnight afterwards hang it—sprinkling it over with a little fine salt. The same pickle will do once again, but not oftener.

ICING JELLIES AND CREAMS.

If you have two or three moulds to ice, get a stone of rough ice, put it into a pail, and sprinkle over a handful of pickling salt, then bury your moulds in it, and leave in the air or a cool place; the ice must come up to within a quarter of an inch of the top of the mould.

They must remain in all day, and the great secret of icing is to turn round the moulds three or four times in the day, so that each part may be equally iced.

MENUS

For one week for four or six people.

Monday.

    Consommé à la Colbert.
    Brill.   Anchovy Sauce.
    Mutton Cutlets à la Soubise.
    Roast Fowl. ⎫
    Bacon broiled round. ⎬ Bread Sauce.
    Petits Gateaux à la Vanille.
    Bloater Toast.

Tuesday.

    Barley Soup.
    Brill au Gratin.
    Rissoles à l'Italienne.
    Small round Roast Beef. ⎫
    Horse-radish Sauce. ⎬
    Yorkshire Pudding. ⎭
    Shape of Semolina, with Cream.
    Soufflé au Fromage.

Wednesday.

    Tapioca Soup.
    Whitings. Plain Butter Sauce.
    Broiled Steaks of Mutton.
    Cold Beef.
    Salad (winter or summer).
    Apple Charlotte.
    Macaroni and Cheese.

Thursday.

    Mutton Broth.
    Sole au vin blanc.
    Timbales.
    Roast Neck of Mutton.
    Omelette aux Fines Herbes.
    Buttered Apples.

Friday.

    Vermicelli Soup.
    Haddock. Oyster Sauce.
    Saddle of Mutton.
    Game.
    Bread and Butter Pudding.

Saturday.

    Pea Soup.

    Alderman's Walk (Broiled or Maitre d' Hotel Sauce).

    Boiled Chickens, with Ham, Tongue, or Bacon.

    Curry of Fish.

    Tapioca Pudding.

Sunday.

    Soup (heated from day before).

    Saddle of Mutton (2nd loin left of Friday, roasted again with buttered paper).

    Mayonnaise Chicken.

    Apple Tart (cold).

MENUS
For eight or ten people.

No. 1.

Potage—Tortue Clair.	Clear Turtle.
Saumon. Sauce Raifort et Hollandaise.	Salmon. Horse-radish, and Dutch Sauce.
Vol au Vent de Homard.	Lobster Vol au Vent.
Cotelettes de Mouton, à la Soubise.	Mutton Cutlets, Soubise Sauce.
Filet de Bœuf. Sauce Madère.	Filet de Bœuf. Madeira Sauce.

Canetons aux petits pois ; or Bécasses.	Ducklings and Peas ; or Woodcocks.
Riz à l' Imperatrice.	Empress Pudding.
Soufflé au Fromage.	Cheese Soufflé.

No. 2.

Potage, Consommé à la Colbert.	Soup (poached eggs).
Merluche. Sauce aux Huitres.	Haddock. Oyster Sauce.
Crème de Volaille.	Crème de Volaille.
Cotelettes de lièvre. Sauce Groseille.	Hare Cutlets. Currant Jelly Sauce.
Selle de Mouton.	Saddle of Mutton.
Homard etuvé.	Stewed Lobster.
Pudding à la Diplomate.	Diplomate Pudding (Iced)
Croutons aux Harengs enfumés.	Bloater Toast.

MENUS
From twelve to sixteen people.

No. 1.

Potage Tortue.	Turtle Soup.
Crème d' Orge.	White Soup.
Filets de Soles à la Horly.	Soles, Tomato Sauce.
Turbot. Sauce Hollandaise.	Turbot. Dutch Sauce.
Rissoles à l' Italienne.	Rissoles.
Vol au Vent aux Huitres.	Oyster Vol au Vent.
Filet de Bœuf aux Truffes.	Filet of Beef, with Truffles.
Poulets aux Champignons.	Chickens with Mushroom Sauce.

Jambon.	Ham.
Aspic de Homard.	Lobster Aspic.
Gelée.	Jelly.
Bavaroise à la Vanille.	Shape of Cream.
Paillettes de Fromage.	Cheese Straws.

No. 2.

Potage—Julienne, à la Reine.	Soup Julienne, à la Reine.
Saumon—Sauce Hollandaise.	Salmon--Dutch Sauce.
Filets de Soles—Sauce Bèarnaise.	Fillets of Soles Bearnaise Sauce.
Huitres en Friture.	Oysters and Bacon.
Cotelettes de Mouton—Sauce Tomate (or, Cotelettes d' Agneau—aux Concombres).	Cutlets of Mutton. Tomato Sauce (or, Lamb Cutlets with Cucumbers).
Filets de Poulets—Sauce Tartare.	Chicken Cutlets—Tartar Sauce.
Roast Beef.	Roast Beef.
Mayonnaise aux Crevettes.	Mayonnaise of Prawns.
Gelée au Rhum.	Rum Jelly.
Pudding Glacé.	Iced Pudding. (To order at Confectioner's).
Sardines à l' Huile.	Sardines with oil.

N.B.—Only one soup need be given for these two last Menus if desired, and one fish, but in that case it must not be salmon.

Receipts for all these dishes will be found in the book, and the above list will serve as a help for other Menus. The dishes must be chosen according to the season.

Much confusion in the serving up of the dinner

will be saved by giving a bill of fare to the cook with each dish numbered ; as for instance :—

No. 1. Soup
2. Fish and Sauces.
Handed round. { 3. Vol au Vent.
(One or two dishes, as the case may be.)
4. Hare Cutlets.
5. Fillet of Beef and Sauce.
6. Ducklings and Peas.
7. Pudding.
8. Cheese Soufflé.

A duplicate to be given to the butler or head waiter.

Up to 10 people it is better to have first the soup, then the fish—then the head dish on the table,—the entrées and sweets only being handed round. But for any number beyond 10, everything must be carved off the table, and a handsome dessert left on all the time of dinner.

SOUPS—(POTAGES).

	PAGE
Brown Stock	30
White Stock	31
To clear Soup	32
Pot au Feu	33
Vermicelli Soup	34
Tapioca Soup	34
Rice Soup	35
Consommé	35
Consommé of Chicken	36
Clear Turtle Soup	36
Bouillon à la Minute	37
Soup à la Française	37
Soup à la Bonne Femme	38
Soup and Bouilli	38
Potage Printanier	39
Potage Julienne	40
Potage Julienne au Consommé	40
French Vegetable Soup	41
Swiss Soup	41
Colbert Soup	42
Hare Soup (clear)	42
Rabbit Soup	43
Beef Tea	43
Clear Ox Tail	44
Thick Ox Tail	44
Mutton Broth	45
Pea Soup	45
German Barley Soup	46
Potage à la Reine,	46
French Onion Soup	46
Cressy Soup	47

SOUPS (POTAGES).

SOUPS.

THE great mistake of English cooks in making soups is the quantity of meat they use, and also omitting to add to the stock a good amount of vegetables, such as turnips, carrots, leeks, onions, &c. Where much meat is used in the house, good white stock ought to be made with the bones and trimmings of the meat used for made dishes. A frequent fault is to put too much salt and pepper in the soup. Let this be avoided.

Stock must always be perfectly cold before putting it away, and kept covered.

It can be kept in winter for two or three days, but in summer it will be necessary to boil it every day.

The meat for soup must always be cut into dice and put into a well buttered soup pot. At first pour over only a small quantity of the water and boil up, stirring round with a spoon for about ten minutes until it forms a thick gravy at the bottom, when add the remainder of the water.

The time for boiling soup depends upon the quality of the meat. As soon as all the juice of the meat is extracted, the soup is ready, and would only be spoilt if the meat were left in longer. The vegetables are not to be added till the stock has been down some little time, and skimmed, and should only be left in till they are done.

BROWN STOCK.

Chop up fine 10 lbs. of beef from the middle of the hock, and also the bones. Add 1 head of celery, 2 carrots, 1 leek, 1 onion, and 2 shalots, and some sweet herbs. To every pound of beef add 2 breakfast cups of water. Let it boil gently for several hours; never let it get to a bubble, or the soup will be white. Skim as soon as it comes to a boil, and then strain. The better it is skimmed the clearer it will be. Vermicelli, rice, tapioca, or macaroni may be added, but must never be boiled with the meat or vegetables.

ANOTHER BROWN STOCK.

If you happen to be out of your stock and want to make soup for the same day, take 3 lbs. of good beef (not soup meat), free from fat and gristle, and cut into small dice. Put into the soup pot with 2 or 3 chicken necks, a head of celery, and a small pinch of salt. Pour over this 2 quarts of boiling water, and boil gently all day, never letting it get to a bubble. Before straining add a cup of cold water, then pass through a hair sieve, or a bit of canvas used for straining milk.

N.B.—The lid of the saucepan must be always closely covered. Add tapioca, vermicelli, or any thickening you like, prepared according to the receipts given.

WHITE STOCK.

Chop up all the bones that you have (cooked and not cooked) very small; if there is meat on the cooked bones so much the better. To every pound of bones add a breakfast cup of cold water, carrots, turnips, and all sorts of herbs. Boil gently all day, then strain. This is a cheap and excellent stock for all kinds of white soup, such as barley, pea soup, mutton broth, &c.

GOOD WHITE STOCK.

Cut up 4 lbs. of knuckle of veal, and put it with the bones and trimmings of poultry, 4 slices of lean ham, into a stewpan which has been rubbed with one ounce of butter. Moisten with half a pint of water, and simmer till the gravy begins to flow. Then add 4 quarts of water, 3 carrots, 2 onions, 1 head of celery, 12 white peppercorns, 2 oz. salt, a blade of mace and a bunch of herbs. Simmer for five hours. Skim and strain carefully through a very fine hair sieve.

N.B.—To make this stronger you can double the quantity of veal, or put in a fowl. A good addition to all white stock is the liquor in which a turkey has been boiled.

TO CLEAR SOUP.

If by some accident the soup is not quite clear use the whites of eggs. For 2 quarts of stock take the whites of 2 eggs carefully separated from their yolks, whisk them together with a half-pint of water, add them gradually to the stock, (which must be just warmed) continuing to whisk them. Place the soup on the fire, and when boiling and well-skimmed, stir well, draw it to the side of the fire, and let it settle until the whites of the eggs become separated. Pass through a fine cloth, when the soup will be clear. All clear soups should be of a light colour, and not taste too strongly of the meat.

N.B.—Soup should never be made of hard water.

POT AU FEU.

See that the fire is carefully made up, and if well made at first, it will not require remaking during the process. It ought to be kept at a gentle regular heat. Take 1½ lb. of beef, bone it, and tie it up with string; take 3 oz. of bones, place them at the bottom of the digester, and the meat on them; add 3½ quarts of water and 1 oz. of salt, and boil. In putting on the cover of the soup-pot, be careful to leave an opening about the width of an inch. As soon as the scum rises, add a quarter pint of cold water, and skim.

Let the broth boil up three times, and skim three times. After this, it ought to be perfectly clear. Wipe the edges carefully, and add the vegetables; this will stop the boiling. As soon as the broth boils up again, draw the soup-pot aside so that a third of it is only over the fire. Place cinders on the fire to subdue the heat, and keep a regular gentle fire for three hours. Then take out the meat and remove all the fat, which can also be done while gently boiling.

VERMICELLI SOUP.

Scald 2 oz. for five minutes in 1¾ pint of water, in which put a teaspoonful of salt. Let it cool, and then pass through a cullender to drain. Pour it into 1¾ pint of boiling stock; stir with a skimmer to prevent the vermicelli getting into lumps. Let it simmer for five minutes on the corner of the range, covering three-quarters of the saucepan. Skim the froth which rises to the surface. The above proportions will give soup for four people. All pastes, such as macaroni or Italian paste, are served in the same manner.

TAPIOCA SOUP.

Into one quart of boiling soup drop gently with one hand 1½ oz. of tapioca, stirring well with a spoon to prevent lumps forming. Then place the saucepan on the corner of the range, and let it simmer for twenty minutes, taking care to keep on the lid of the saucepan to prevent a scum forming on the surface; skim and serve. The above proportions are for soup for four people.

N.B.—The French tapioca prepared by Groult is the best.

RICE SOUP.

Wash a good ounce of Carolina rice in three waters; scald in 1¾ pint of water, stirring it carefully. Let it get cool, and drain it. Pour into one quart of boiling soup, stirring it to mix well. Leave the saucepan three-quarters covered for twenty-five minutes at the corner of the range to give the rice time to swell. Skim and serve. The above proportions are for soup for four people.

CONSOMMÉ.

Take 2½ lbs. knuckle of veal, 2½ lbs. shin of beef, 5 lbs. lean beef (cut from the middle of the hock), and a good fowl. Cut into pieces, and put them in the soup pot which must be *well* cleaned, pour over 6 quarts of water (which will make 4 quarts of soup). Simmer over a slow fire for several hours, then add 2 carrots, celery, 2 cloves, thyme, laurel leaf, and salt, and when these are done, pass the soup through a tammy, and skim.

N.B.—A second stock can be made by pouring fresh water on the ingredients, add salt, and boil for two hours.

CONSOMMÉ OF CHICKEN.

After making the consommé, skim and clarify with the fillets of 2 chickens, pass through a napkin, and keep for use.

TURTLE SOUP (Clear).

Get dried turtle (which is to be had at 10s. per lb.), ½ lb. will be sufficient for soup for 12 people. Soak it for three days in cold water, changing the water twice a-day, then take 5 quarts of consommé and let the turtle simmer gently in it. When quite soft take out the turtle and again clear the soup, then cut it into large squares, and put them into the tureen, into which pour the soup boiling (having previously added to it a pint of Madeira).

FRENCH RECEIPT for BOUILLON à la Minute.

Take 1 lb. lean beef, and half a fowl boned. Pound all together and put with some salt (about two teaspoonsful) into a saucepan, with $2\frac{1}{2}$ pints of water, and let it boil over a good fire, stirring gently. As soon as it begins to boil add carrots, turnips, onions, leeks, and celery, all chopped up. Boil twenty minutes—strain, and serve.

SOUP à la Francaise.

(This is a most useful receipt for daily use.)

Take 3 lbs. of lean beef, put in a saucepan holding 5 quarts of water. When it comes to a boil take it off the fire and remove the scum, then fill the pot with every kind of soup vegetable, such as celery, parsnips, carrots, turnips, leeks, and onions, taking care not to let it flavour too strongly of the celery and parsnips. Stew quietly all day; at night strain into an earthen pan. In the morning remove the fat and clear it with the whites of two eggs, not stirring it while boiling. It ought only to boil for about two minutes, then draw it from the fire and let it stand at the corner of the range for quarter of an hour, then strain through a fine cloth. Have ready some very finely shred vegetables, carrots, turnips, peas, cauliflower, etc., boiled separately from the stock in a little water or stock; when quite done, throw them into the soup and give them one boil.

SOUP à la BONNE FEMME.

Shred 12 green leaves of a lettuce very fine. Fry them in a little butter, keeping them well stirred for ten minutes. Add a quart of good stock and boil for half an hour. Then mix in the yolks of 6 eggs, half a pint of cream, a very little pounded sugar and salt. Stir quickly, and only just let it thicken without boiling, or it will curdle, which would spoil the soup.

SOUP AND BOUILLI.

Put in the digester a shin of beef cut into pieces, the bones and remains of meat, necks of chickens, &c. Add 7 or 8 pints of water, when it has begun to boil, 2 or 3 carrots, 1 head of celery, 3 leeks, an onion stuck with 3 cloves, half a laurel leaf, a little thyme, and some salt. The soup will take 5 hours boiling. After it has been down for two hours put 3 lbs. of beef in the same pot, and in 3 hours it will be ready to serve, with vegetables separately boiled. The soup may be skimmed and strained (vermicelli added according to the receipt already given, if desired).

POTAGE PRINTANIER.

April, May, and June are the best months for this soup, as young vegetables are required.

Cut into all sorts of shapes young carrots, turnips, small onions, asparagus tops, cauliflowers divided into little bunches, green peas, and French beans, each to be separately scalded with a little salt and boiling water, and then put into cold water. Then take some boiling consommé, throw in a head of celery, first cook the turnips and carrots, then the onions; when they are done add the other vegetables (which have been already more than three-quarters done in the scalding), and take care not to let them break. The peas and beans ought to be very green, and the soup very clear and rich. Add the smallest quantity of white sugar.

POTAGE JULIENNE.

Cut into short thin lengths carrots, turnips, leeks, and celery. Fry them in some butter. Add some stock (or water if for Soupe Maigre), and boil gently for three hours. When it boils add young peas, lettuce, and some chopped chervil (the points of the leaves), and sorrel. Add a very little sugar. During the months of January, February, and March the vegetables are always hard.

POTAGE JULIENNE AU CONSOMMÉ.

Take the red part of 4 carrots, 4 turnips, 3 branches of a head of celery, 3 onions, 6 leeks. Cut all these vegetables into narrow strips, put them in a saucepan, add 9 ounces of butter and a teaspoonful of sugar, till the above vegetables are well browned, then add 4 quarts of consommé, and simmer 3 hours. Ten minutes before serving add some lettuce and sorrel which have been scalded, and cut like the other vegetables. When ready to serve, skim and strain.

FRENCH VEGETABLE SOUP.

Take 5 small carrots, 3 turnips, 3 small leeks, cut them into small pieces, add one pint of peas, put all into 4 quarts of boiling water, and let them boil over a slow fire for three and a-half hours, then add 2 ozs. of butter, and strain through a sieve, after which boil again for five or six minutes. Put two yolks of eggs into the tureen and add gradually the boiling soup, with a little cream.

SWISS SOUP.

For six persons take about a common dishful of spinach. Add a handful of chervil, then pound 2 cabbage stalks, slice 3 or 4 onions, stalks, and marjoram. Mince them together very fine, and press out the juice till the vegetables are quite dry. Heat some butter in a pan, and let the vegetables steep in it until soft, but not too long, or else they will get watery. When thoroughly steeped, stir in a cupful of flour, and pour over it as much water (or broth) as will make the necessary quantity of soup. Add a little salt, and boil a good quarter of an hour. Before serving, put in the tureen the yolks of 2 eggs beaten up with a spoonful of cream, and add the boiling soup.

COLBERT SOUP.

Take some good consommé, and serve in it poached eggs, one for each person, prepared as follows:—Put a little water in the frying pan, add a pinch of salt, and half a wine glass of vinegar; when the water boils break in the eggs, and cover the frying pan with a lid. In two minutes take off from the fire. If the white covers the yolk with a solid top the egg is done. Put into an earthen dish not quite three pints of tepid water, raise each egg with the draining spoon, and put them in one by one, drain them, and trim neatly the outer surface of the white, to give them an oval shape. Put them into the soup tureen, and pour the boiling soup over. Great care is needed in poaching the eggs.

CLEAR HARE SOUP.

The fillets of the hare will make cutlets, but keep the body and the blood for soup (one hare will make three pints of soup), and put them into a stew-pan with three pints of cold water, peppercorns, and some onions which have been fried in the pan with some thyme. Boil all day. Skim well. Strain through a hair sieve, and let it stand till next day, when clear it with egg shells and onion peels. Before serving add a little port wine. It ought to be as clear as sherry.

RABBIT SOUP.

Cut up the rabbit small. Colour some butter. Take 6 onions and brown the meat in them, stirring carefully. Then add a heaped spoonful of flour, some stock or water, a little chopped parsley, salt, and 2 laurel leaves. When the meat is tender, pour the broth through a sieve, heat it again on the fire and boil as much sago in it as will thicken it.

BEEF TEA.

Take 2 lbs. good juicy lean beef. Free it entirely from every bit of skin and fat, chop it up very fine, and put into an earthen jar with a cover. The jar must be just the size to hold the whole quantity loosely, and *without being pressed down*. Add as much cold water as the jar will hold, which will be about a pint and a half, and sprinkle a little salt on it. Put the jar into an oven, where it must remain from eight to twelve hours, (the oven being of a moderate heat the whole time,) until every drop of juice is extracted from the meat. When done strain, and let it stand till cold. Heat as required in the bainmarie.

CLEAR OX-TAIL SOUP.

Stew down three ox-tails in plain gravy, add three quarts good well-flavoured beef stock. Clear the soup, and flavour with cayenne pepper and port wine. Cut the tails into pieces and stew them ten minutes in the soup before serving.

THICK OX-TAIL SOUP.

Take 2 ox-tails, cut them in pieces, and put in a saucepan with 2 quarts of water, and let simmer till well done. Then mix together ½ lb. of butter, sufficient flour to thicken; 2 sliced onions (previously fried in butter), and a bunch of herbs tied in a piece of muslin. Boil all together half an hour, then strain through a fine sieve.

Cut some carrots and turnips into shapes, cook them separately, and when the soup is ready to be served, throw in the vegetables and mix all together. Make up the quantity of soup required by the addition of good stock. This soup is better made the day before it is wanted, as when cold the fat can be removed before adding the other ingredients.

MUTTON BROTH.

To every pound of scrag of mutton put two breakfast cups of water; add pearl barley, carrots, turnips, thyme, and onions, and boil for five or six hours. When it comes to a boil, skim, and continue this, as the grease rises. Add a little parsley just before serving.

PEA SOUP.

To every quart of white stock add one large tablespoonful of Symington's pea flour; blend it smoothly and let it boil for about ten minutes, stirring all the time. Serve very hot, with squares of fried bread on a separate plate.

GERMAN BARLEY SOUP (Gerstenschleim).

Take one pound of fine barley, and fry with 6 oz. fresh butter for a few minutes. Then pour over a quart of white stock, and boil slowly for three or four hours. Pass through a hair sieve, add the yolk of an egg and some cream, and serve. The addition of thick cream and the yolks of two eggs will make this soup Crème d' Orge.

POTAGE à la Reine.

Roast a fowl, skin it, pound the flesh, and pass through a tammy. Break the bones and boil them with some rice till it is tender, then pass it also through a tammy, mix it with the chicken, and put down both into some stock (white if possible), and when done add some cream, and serve with sippets fried in butter. The soup ought to be as smooth as cream.

FRENCH ONION SOUP.

Take rather better than ¾ lb. onions, peel them, and cut them crossways in very thin slices, all the same size and thickness, so that they may be equally cooked. Parboil them for ten minutes in boiling water, and drain. Put 1 oz. butter into a saucepan, and let the onions colour over a quick fire. When they have got a light colour add 1 oz. flour, leave it for two minutes on the fire. Add $1\frac{3}{4}$ pint of water, two pinches of salt, and the same of pepper— stir on the fire till the first boiling, leave it for five minutes by the side of the fire. Put in the tureen 2 oz. bread, and 1 oz. of butter, stir lightly with a spoon to melt the butter, and serve.

CRESSY SOUP (Maigre).

Put four good carrots, a large onion, and half a stick of celery into a saucepan of boiling water. Boil slowly till the carrots are quite soft. (Should it boil away add more boiling water.) Rub the carrots through a tammy, and put them back into the soup. Boil slowly till of the proper consistency. Season with pepper and salt, and serve with fried bread cut in dice and fried in butter or oil.

FISH—(With Sauces).

INDEX.

	PAGE
Boiled Soles,	53
Melted Butter,	53
Richer Melted Butter,	54
Sauce Impératrice,	54
Parsley Sauce,	55
Shrimp Sauce,	55
French Mode of Serving Fried Fish,	55
Boiled Haddock	56
Oyster Sauce,	56
Egg Sauce,	57
Anchovy Sauce,	57
Rich Anchovy Sauce,	57
Brill,	58
Dutch Sauce,	58
Turbot,	59
Lobster Sauce,	60
Brill or Turbot au Gratin,	61
Kedgeree,	62
Fish served with Curry Powder,	62
Salmon,	62
Sauce Raifort (Horse-radish),	63
Sauce Béarnaise,	63
Salmon Rissoles,	63
Sole au Vin Blanc,	64
Boiled Fillets of Soles,	64
Fillets of Soles à la Horly,	64

INDEX.

	PAGE
Tomato Sauce,	65
Fillets of Soles and Anchovies,	66
Fillets of Mackerel,	66
Mackerel—Maitre d' Hotel Sauce,	67
Fresh Herrings—Mustard Sauce,	67
Skate (Raie au beurre noir),	68
Water Souché	68

FISH—(With Sauces.)

BOILED SOLES.

Soles for boiling must be large. Well wash and clean them, remove the fins, and put the soles into a fish kettle with salt and water. Let them boil slowly and simmer until done, when serve on a napkin with the white side uppermost, with melted butter or shrimp sauce.

MELTED BUTTER.

Have your saucepan very clean; put into it 2½ oz. fresh butter, with two tablespoonsful of water, and shake it over a clear fire one way until it boils; make it quite hot, but be careful not to colour it; well whisk the yolks of two eggs, pour them to the butter, beating them all the while. Add a squeeze of lemon juice, and if you like, a few capers.

RICHER MELTED BUTTER.

Take about half-a-pound of butter, put it with salt and pepper and two tablespoonsful of lemon-juice into a saucepan, which place on the fire, stir with a wooden spoon, and when melted to half its quantity take it off the fire, and continue stirring till it is entirely dissolved. By not melting the whole of it on the fire the sauce will be more creamy, and a fresher taste than if it had been the whole time on the fire.

SAUCE IMPÉRATRICE.

Mix some flour with a little water (in the proportion of one tablespoonful for every two persons), adding salt, pepper, and a little vinegar. Put on the fire till the flour is well mixed, then add butter (allow for each person 1 oz.) in tiny pieces, beating well all the time, and take care that each piece is well incorporated before you put in the next. Keep the sauce near the fire. It must never be allowed to boil. The greater the quantity of butter the better and richer the sauce will be. For all kinds of boiled fish this is an excellent sauce.

PARSLEY SAUCE

Is made like butter sauce; the parsley to be chopped and thrown into the boiling water just before mixing with the flour.

SHRIMP SAUCE.

Mix a teaspoonful of essence of anchovies and a pinch of cayenne with half-a-pint of melted butter; add a pint of picked shrimps to the melted butter when boiling; then set it on one side of the fire till the shrimps are heated through, but do not let it boil again. Add a very little piece of lemon.

FRENCH METHOD OF SERVING FRIED FISH.

Let the dripping be boiling hot—then put your fish in, and when done, serve on a hot dish in which is previously placed a small bit of butter, and scatter finely-chopped herbs over the fish. No butter sauce is required when the fish is done this way.

N.B.—Be careful to dry and flour the fish before putting it into the dripping. Small soles, flounders, and large whiting are also done this way.

BOILED HADDOCK.

Clean and wash thoroughly, then scrape, put in the fish kettle and simmer gently. You must put enough water to cover the fish. Put salt in the water—$\frac{1}{4}$ lb. to a gallon is a good proportion. Serve with oyster or anchovy sauce. If the fish be salted, serve with egg sauce.

OYSTER SAUCE.

Allow four oysters to each person.

Open the oysters carefully, and save the liquor. Strain it into a clean lined saucepan, put in the oysters, and let them just come to the boiling point. Take them off the fire immediately, and put the whole into a basin. Strain the liquor and mix with it sufficient milk to make half a pint altogether. Take (to make the melted butter) 1 teaspoonful of flour and 2 oz. of butter, and mix them smoothly together on a plate; put it into the lined saucepan, and pour in one-third of a pint of milk. Keep stirring it *one way* over a sharp fire, and let it boil quickly for a minute or two.

When ready, and very smooth, put in the oysters (previously bearded). Set it by the side of the fire till heated through, but do not allow it to boil, or the oysters will get hard. Cream, instead of milk, makes this sauce delicious.

EGG SAUCE.

Make some good melted butter. Then take some eggs (the number must depend upon the quantity required), boil till hard, then soak them in cold water. When quite cold take off the shells and cut the eggs into large dice, laying them in a sauceboat, previously well heated. Pour the melted butter very hot over the eggs, and serve.

RICH ANCHOVY SAUCE.

This is a most excellent sauce when you do not want the expense of oyster or lobster sauce, and eats well with all boiled and fried fish.

ANCHOVY SAUCE (less Rich).

Stir three dessert-spoonsful of Burgess' essence of anchovy into half a pint of good melted butter. Season with a little cayenne, and boil it up for a minute or two.

D

Bone four Gorgona anchovies, pound them in a mortar to paste with 1 oz. of butter. Heat ½ pint of good melted butter, stir in the pounded anchovies and a little cayenne. Simmer for three or four minutes, and add a squeeze of lemon juice.

BRILL.

Take 4 oz. of salt to each gallon of water, and add a tablespoonful of vinegar. Thoroughly clean and remove the scales. Do not cut off the fins. Rub with the juice of lemon and a little salt. Set in a fish kettle, covering it with the salt and water and vinegar.

Bring it gradually to boil, and simmer for ten or twenty minutes, according to size.

Skim well. Serve with Dutch sauce.

DUTCH SAUCE.

Put into a quart saucepan two tablespoonsful of vinegar, seasoned with a little salt and white pepper; reduce it on the fire till you have about a dessertspoonful of vinegar. Take it from the fire, adding two tablespoonsful of cold water, and the yolks of two eggs, taking care not to leave any white. Put again on a gentle fire, stirring with a wooden spoon. As soon as the yolks begin to set, take from the fire. Divide ¼ lb. of butter into five heaps. Now add one heap to the eggs, and stir with the spoon till melted, then put on the fire for a minute, adding the second heap. Do this till all the heaps of butter are melted, but be careful that one heap is dissolved before the other is added. After having mixed the third heap, pour into the saucepan a tablespoonful of cold water, to prevent the sauce from curdling. When all the butter is used, add another tablespoonful of cold water, and even more should you find it necessary.

TURBOT.

First empty the fish, wash the inside, rubbing a little salt over it. Put into water to cleanse it, and change the water several times. Put plenty of cold water into a fish kettle, adding to each gallon 4 oz. of salt, and a very small quantity of saltpetre. Let this dissolve. Make an incision in the skin of the back nearly to the bone, to prevent the white side from cracking. Do not cut off the fins. Place the turbot on the fish plate, and put it into the water, which should quite cover it. Boil slowly, and skim the water carefully. Simmer gently for about half an hour, and when done, lift up the fish plate and let it drain.

Serve with lobster or any other of the sauces.

LOBSTER SAUCE.

Choose a middling sized hen lobster. Pick the meat from the shells, and cut into small square pieces. Put the spawn into a mortar with half an oz. of butter, and pound quite smooth. Rub through a hair sieve, and cover till wanted.

Make the following melted butter:—

Mix 1 tablespoonful of flour and $\frac{1}{2}$ gill of water to a smooth batter, carefully rubbing down with the back of a spoon any lumps. Put into a saucepan with $\frac{1}{4}$ lb. of fresh butter, a little salt, and half a spoonful of white vinegar. Let it thicken on the fire. Simmer just one minute, but do not allow it to boil.

Put into $\frac{3}{4}$ pint of the above melted butter one tablespoonful of anchovy sauce and the butter (with the spawn). Salt and cayenne to taste, and 3 tablespoonsful of cream. Mix all well before you add the lobster, then put it in until thoroughly hot, but do not allow it to boil.

BRILL OR TURBOT, heated up next day,
(au Gratin.)

Take the remains of fish left from the previous day, pick from the bones, and warm gently in salt and water. Then make separately the following sauce:—Mix very smoothly 2 tablespoonsful of flour with 1 quart of milk, a spoonful of salt, and not quite a saltspoonful of pepper. Stir over the fire till tolerably thick. Then lift to the side of the fire, stir in ¼ lb. of butter, and pass through a sieve.

Cover the bottom of the dish with this sauce, lay on it some of the fish, sprinkling with white pepper and salt, then more sauce, then more fish, till all is used. Sprinkle bread crumbs over it, and bake in a hot oven for twenty minutes. Brown and serve in the same dish. A soufflé tin is the best for this dish. Serve with a frill round.

FISH AND RICE (Kedgeree).

Take fish left from the previous day, chop fine, with two hard boiled eggs, and mix well together. Add a teacupful of well-boiled rice, a little white pepper, cayenne, and salt. Put all into a saucepan, adding two or three ounces of fresh butter, cut in bits. Stir over the fire, and serve hot.

N.B.—This is also very good for breakfast.

FISH served with Curry Powder.

Take any fish left from dinner, sprinkle curry powder over it, let it remain all night, and broil the next morning for breakfast.

SALMON.

Scale, empty, and wash carefully in warm water, in order to keep the colour and set the curd. Do not leave any blood inside.

Boil rapidly in salt and water (to the proportion of 4 oz. to one gallon of water) for a couple of minutes, taking off the scum as it rises. Then put in the salmon and boil gently till thoroughly done. Take it off the fish plate, drain, and serve with either lobster sauce or Bearnaise, or with iced horse-radish sauce, of which put a small lump on one side of the plate, and Dutch sauce (hot) on the other.

SAUCE RAIFORT (Horse-radish).

Grate some horse-radish very fine. Take two tablespoonsful, and mix into it a good tablespoonful of cream. Then beat up to a thick cream two oz. of fresh butter, and mix all lightly together, flavouring with a few drops of Tarragon vinegar, and set it on ice. It should be of the consistency of iced cream.

SAUCE BÉARNAISE.

Take some brown sauce, flavour with a bunch of herbs, thicken slightly, add some capers and a small clove of garlic. Brown with French browning ball.

SALMON RISSOLES.

Take some cold salmon, and make into rissoles à l' Italienne. For variety, instead of shaping them into cutlets, they can be made into round balls, and served with Dutch sauce or French melted butter.

SOLE AU VIN BLANC.

Put into the baking-dish some butter, pepper, and salt, and som efinely pounded bread crumbs, and a large sole. Add a glass of Sauterne wine, parsley, mushrooms, and any seasoning you like, scatter some bread crumbs over the surface, and bake in the oven till done. Remove carefully from the dish, and pour over it the sauce, to which, if necessary, add a little more wine.

BOILED FILLETS OF SOLES, with Parsley and Butter.

Make a bèchamel with two tablespoonful of flour to one pint of milk and 3 oz. of butter, and give it one boil. Then boil a bunch of parsley separately, pass it through a fine sieve. Then prepare the fillets of soles, roll and mix in the above sauce, taking care that it does not boil.

FILLETS OF SOLES, à la Horly.

Raise the flesh off the fish with a long thin knife, and cut in the shape of a long pear.

Make a pickle of lemon-juice, pepper, salt, oil, onions in slices, parsley in branches; let them remain in it for an hour; half an hour before serving drain through a cloth, dip into flour, and then fry a light golden colour, serving with Tomato sauce in a separate boat.

TOMATO SAUCE.

Take out the seeds and remove the stalks from six tomatos, put them into a stew-pan, with half an ounce of celery, 1 oz. of butter, 1 oz. of bacon, half an onion cut into slices, a bay leaf, a little thyme, pepper, salt, and cayenne. Stew gently until tender, then stir in a little flour, moisten with half a pint of broth, boil for five or six minutes, strain through a sieve, and then put back into the stew-pan to simmer until rather thick. If you cannot get fresh tomatos the preserved pulp is to be had at Crosse and Blackwell's, and can be used according to the following receipt :—

Put into a small stew-pan six sliced shalots, a bay leaf, thyme, and a wineglassful of vinegar. Boil gently for five minutes, then add about $\frac{1}{4}$ lb. of the pulp, 1 oz. of glaze, a teaspoonful of anchovy, and a lump of sugar. Stir over the fire until the whole has boiled for five minutes, then press through a pointed tin strainer into a small saucepan for use.

FILLETS OF SOLES AND ANCHOVIES.

Raise the fillets off a small sole. Take off the skins, and season with salt and pepper. Fry with a tablespoonful of olive oil, then put a weight over to flatten them. Clean 4 anchovies and wash out the salt. Cut each fillet into lengths of four. Pare the fillets of soles, and cut them into the same length as the anchovies. Range in a china dish alternately with the anchovies.

Put into a small earthen pan four tablespoonsful of oil and one of Tarragon vinegar, with one pickled chili minced very fine. Mix, and put it over the anchovies and soles.

FILLETS OF MACKEREL—Dutch Sauce.

Cut the mackerel in two, raise the fillets, and shape them in the form of a long pear, then put them into a buttered frying-pan. Season with pepper and salt. Cover with butter, and wrap in a round of buttered paper. Fry and dress them in a circle. Serve with Dutch Sauce.

MACKEREL—Maitre d'Hotel Sauce.

Clean and wipe the mackerel, split down the back, season with pepper and salt, and put into a dish with a little oil. Shake them about in the oil, so that the skin of the fish is covered all over. Cook over a moderate fire, on the gridiron, then arrange on a dish, and place in the split of the back a maitre d' hotel butter, which is composed of a little minced parsley kneaded with fresh butter, with lemon juice, pepper, and salt added.

FRESH HERRINGS, with Mustard Sauce.

Wipe and clean the herrings, score, and put them on a plate with oil, to which add pepper and salt, and saturate the herrings with the oil. Then broil and serve with the following sauce:—Mix some flour, butter, and water, and boil for one or two minutes. It must be rather thick. After the boiling, add butter, lemon-juice, and mustard. Stir together without allowing it to boil, and serve with the herrings. This sauce requires a great deal of butter.

SKATE (Raie au Beurre Noir).

Well wash the skate, divide the body from the two wings, cut it into small square pieces, and remove the thick glutinous skin. Put into the fish kettle with boiling water, to which add a wineglass of vinegar, some thyme, and a laurel leaf. Let it boil two or three minutes, an dserve with the following sauce poured over it.

Put a good lump of fresh butter into a saucepan and let it brown well; then take it away from the fire and let it get cold.

Put in another saucepan three tablespoonsful of vinegar and two pinches of pepper. Reduce it to two tablespoonsful, then take the saucepan off the fire. See that the melted butter is perfectly cold, then pass it through a strainer into the saucepan with the vinegar, mix well, and heat it, taking great care that it does not boil.

WATER SOUCHE.

Stew 6 trout in a quart of water with some parsley leaves and roots till the fish are boiled to rags. Then pulp what remains through a sieve. Stew some fresh trout in this liquor with more parsley and some slices of carrot. Serve in a deep dish with brown bread and butter.

ENTRÉES.

INDEX.

	PAGE
Mutton Cutlets, with Fried Potatoes,	76
,, ,, Sauce Italienne,	77
,, ,, aux Coucombres,	77
,, ,, à la Maintenon,	78
,, ,, à la Reforme,	78
,, ,, à la Soubise,	79
,, ,, aux Marrons (Chestnuts),	80
Haricot of Mutton	81
Filets Mignons	81
Filets Mignons Piques,	82
Thickening for Sauces,	82
French Thickening for Sauces,	83
Sauce Poivrade,	84
Sauce Piquante,	84
Lamb Cutlets, aux petits pois,	85
Lamb's Sweetbreads in Scollops,	85
White Sauce,	85
Lamb Cutlets, aux coucombres,	86
Vol au Vent of Lobster	86
,, ,, Shrimps or Prawns,	86
,, ,, Oysters,	87
,, ,, à la Bèchamel,	87
Coquilles de Volaille,	88
Beef Scollops,	88
Filets de Bœuf,	89
Beef Steak à la Milanaise,	90
Rissole Cutlets,	91
Truffle Sauce,	91
Quenelle of Rabbit,	92

INDEX.

	PAGE
Poulet à la Crapandine,	92
Chicken Cutlets,	93
Chicken Cutlets à la Tartare,	93
Broiled Chicken,	94
Bombay Curry,	94
Rice for Curry,	95
Egg Curry,	96
Chicken and Tomato Sauce,	96
Chicken à la Josephine,	96
Chickens à la Brèsilienne,	97
Poulet au Riz,	98
Poulet au Blanc,	98
Crème de Volaille,	99
China Chilo,	100
Timbales,	100
Kebobs,	101
German Veal Cutlets,	101
Veal Scallops,	102
Rognons à la Brochette,	103
Hare Cutlets,	104
Sauce Groseille,	105
Rabbit Cutlets,	105
Salmi of Pheasant,	106
Salmi of Wild Duck,	106
Larded Sweetbreads,	107
Riz de Veau en Caisses	107
Calf's Liver,	108
Pigeons,	109

ENTRÉES.

No matter how well the entrées are cooked, their appearance is spoilt if they are not nicely served up. Cutlets for instance (unless there are a sufficient number to keep them in a circle standing upright), are often difficult to arrange; and mashed potatoes as a centre on which to rest them are often resorted to, This at once stamps the dish as common. I have found that a French roll (with the top cut off and scooped out so as to allow truffles, peas, &c., to be put inside), make a very pretty centre for cutlets, fillets of chicken, &c., each cutlet being trimmed with a frill of paper, and a sauce served round. For variety the hare cutlets, with currant jelly sauce, may have a boiled beetroot in the centre. This and the roll are of course only for effect, and not to be cut. For ten or twelve people there should always be duplicates of each entrée. Remember that one entrée ought to be *white* sauce and material, and the other *brown*; and if there is a vol au vent of lobster, the second entrée ought to be mutton cutlets with a brown sauce, and if the entrée is mutton, the *pièce de resistance* must be beef, and the savoury dish must not be of lobster, because the vol au vent is made of lobster.

PLAIN MUTTON CUTLETS with Fried Potatoes.

Trim twelve of equal thickness, dust them with salt. Put some clarified butter into a frying pan, *sautez* the cutlets, cover them with a round of buttered paper, when done drain them, glaze and dress them in a circle on the dish, put the fried potatoes in the middle, and serve either with plain gravy, tomato, or Italian sauce (for the two latter without potatoes).

To fry the potatoes proceed as follows:— Peel six potatoes, cut them on the breadth into narrow strips or into round balls. Put into the frying-pan about 2 lbs. of dripping, melt it over a quick fire, and throw in the potatoes. Stir from time to time with the skimmer, so that the potatoes are equally cooked; from eight to ten minutes will be enough, then drain.

SAUCE à l' Italienne.

Put in a small stew-pan a dessert-spoonful of very finely chopped shalots, the same quantity of salad oil, a bay leaf, and thyme; and stir this over the fire in order to fry the shalot without letting it colour. Then add a good table-spoonful of chopped mushrooms, a glass of sherry, a glass of mushroom catsup, a teaspoonful of essence of Anchovy, half a pint of stock, and one oz. of brown thickening. Stir over the fire until the sauce boils, and then allow the scum to rise by the side of the fire for ten minutes, then skim and pour into a stew-pan for use.

MUTTON CUTLETS with Cucumbers.

Chop some parsley and shalots very fine, and put them in a little melted butter, dip in the cutlets, and then in bread crumbs. Put them in the frying pan, and fry a fine light brown. Cut two cucumbers into four quarters, removing all the seeds; cut them in oval shapes about one inch long; boil them in half vinegar and water till tender. Make a sauce with the trimmings of the cutlets, some minced shalots and herbs. Put the cucumbers into the sauce and make them very hot. Serve in the centre of the dish.

MUTTON CUTLETS à la Maintenon.

Take them from the neck or loin, about $1\frac{1}{2}$ lb. and chop each bone short. Trim them neatly, and put them into a stewpan with a piece of butter and a little finely chopped thyme and parsley. Season with pepper and salt, fry lightly, and then take them out to cool, after which take some fresh chopped parsley and bread crumbs, spread them evenly over the cutlets with a knife, wrap each in buttered paper, and broil over a clear fire. Serve up in the papers with gravy in a tureen.

MUTTON CUTLETS à la Reforme.

Take some truffles, the red part of carrots boiled, some hard boiled whites of eggs, a little of the lean of ham and the same of tongue, and some green gherkins, and shred them into neat strippets half-an-inch long. Make them hot in a basin in the screen while you prepare the following sauce:—Cut up into small dice some lean bacon, and an equal quantity each of carrots, celery and onion, and a little mace. Fry all in a small stewpan with a piece of butter the size of a walnut until the whole becomes well-browned, add a wineglassful of vinegar and half the quantity of catsup, and a teaspoonful of essence of anchovy. When this is reduced to half, add half a pint of brown sauce, and a glass of sherry. Let the sauce boil gently to throw up the grease, and strain through a sieve.

Toss the chips lightly in this sauce, and pour all over nicely prepared cutlets.

MUTTON CUTLETS à la Soubise—Excellent.

Cut six chops about an inch thick off a neck of mutton, trim off most of the fat, put them into a frying pan with 2 ozs. of butter, cover up close in the oven for eight minutes, then turn them. Strain the butter off, and add a half-pint of clear gravy, and let them simmer gently for half-an-hour. When ready to dish up, glaze them, and pour the brown gravy round them, with soubise sauce in the centre.

WHITE SOUBISE SAUCE.

Boil three good sized onions till quite tender, strain the water well from them, then pass through a tammy or hair sieve, add a quarter pint of cream and a lump of glaze about the size of a nutmeg, and thicken with a tablespoonful of flour. Boil for five minutes, stirring well or it will burn.

MUTTON CUTLETS Purée aux Marrons (Chestnuts).

Take a good handful of chestnuts, strip them of the brown skin, then put them into boiling water, when the second skin will come off. Put into a saucepan a little stock (veal is the best) to which add a piece of butter, a little sugar, and salt. Stew the chestnuts in this till quite tender, then put them into another saucepan. The purée ought to be pretty thick, but if you find it requires thinning, add a little more stock, then stir in a little more butter, which must be very fresh. This sauce is served like the soubise, round nicely broiled cutlets, or serve separately in a boat.

HARICOT OF MUTTON.

(French Receipt.)

Take from 2 to 3 lbs. of chops, put them into a stewpan. Add butter, and two or three onions cut into thin slices, fry all together till nicely browned. Make a roux with a little stock and flour, and add it to the meat. Cook the vegetables first by themselves, and then add to the other ingredients about half-an-hour before the meat is quite done. Cut into strips 2 carrots, 2 turnips and some celery; when half done put them into the stewpan with the meat. Serve very hot.

FILETS MIGNONS.

(The Filet Mignon is the fillet that lies under the saddle, and often called in English the "Alderman's walk").

Cut the fillet into 12 pieces, flatten them with a beater, removing the skin and the nerves. Trim them in the shape of a long pear. Lard and put them for 24 hours into a pickle of oil, onions, and a little parsley. When about to be cooked drain on a napkin. Butter a pan and put them in. Moisten with a little broth, without entirely covering them. When done, glaze and serve.

Arrange them in a circle, with the roll centre, which fill with chopped mushrooms, and serve with a Poivrade or Piquante sauce.

N.B.—The fillets may be served plainly broiled with pepper and salt.

FILETS MIGNONS LARDED.

Raise the fillets in length and shape them round, larding them at the top. Put some slices of bacon in a saucepan with some carrots, onions, 2 cloves, a bunch of parsley, some chives, thyme, and a laurel leaf. Place the fillets in this seasoning, then cover them with two sheets of buttered paper; add a tablespoonful of stock. Put it on the fire at the end of an hour, put some fire on the lid to glaze the fillets. When ready to serve, drain, and serve with cucumber, chicory, or any dressing preferred.

THICKENING FOR SAUCES.

Melt one pound of butter in a stew-pan upon a slow fire. Remove the scum with a spoon, and then pour off the clarified butter into another clean stew-pan. Add to this one pound of sifted flour well mixed with a wooden spoon. Continue stirring over a slow fire for about an hour, till of a very light brown colour, then pour into an earthen pan to be kept ready for use.

FRENCH THICKENING.

Put into a saucepan ¾ lb. of fresh butter. When melted add 4 or 5 spoonsful of flour. Stir the butter and flour with a wooden spoon over a gentle fire till of a light brown colour. If required to be darker, thin it with broth, which must be poured boiling hot over the sauce, which must be allowed to stand till cold. Place it on the corner of the oven for nearly an hour. Skim the grease and the scum which form on the top, and then put on a brisk fire to reduce the same. Then take up the sauce with a spoon, and work backwards and forwards till well blended, but it must not be too thick. Then pass through a tammy, and add a few small pieces of butter.

SAUCE POIVRADE.

Cut up the following into very small square pieces :—1 oz. lean ham or bacon, the same each of carrot, celery, and onion, a bay leaf and thyme, 20 peppercorns, and a bit of mace.

Fry in a small stew-pan with a piece of butter the size of a walnut, until the whole becomes well browned; add a wineglassful of vinegar and half that quantity of mushroom catsup, and a teaspoonful of anchovy. When reduced to half add half a pint of brown sauce, a few spoonsful of good stock, and a wineglassful of sherry. Let the sauce boil gently by the side of the fire, and having removed the grease, strain through a sieve into a small stew-pan for use.

SAUCE PIQUANTE.

Put into a stew-pan gherkins, capers, and shalots, all chopped as fine as dust, a tablespoonful of each, with a little pepper and a wineglassful of vinegar. To boil about four minutes, then add rather better than half a pint of good stock, 1 oz. of brown thickening, a small bit of glaze, and a teaspoonful of anchovy. Boil and skim.

LAMB CUTLETS with Green Peas or Beans.

Take them from off the best end of the neck; brush each cutlet over with well beaten yolk of egg; sprinkle them with fine bread crumbs seasoned with pepper and salt. After this dip them separately into a little clarified butter. Sprinkle more crumbs over them, and fry, turning occasionally. Lay them before the fire to drain. Then dish them in a circle, with peas or French beans in the centre, and serve with the following white sauce.

WHITE SAUCE.

Boil two onions in one pint and a half of milk until reduced to a pint. Take out the onions; press them so as to extract all the juice. Stir into the milk whilst boiling 2 oz. of fine flour mixed in a ¼ pint of cold milk (or cream). Stir over the fire until it simmers, and is as thick as rich cream; add salt and cayenne. Put in 2 oz. butter, and when melted serve the sauce.

LAMB CUTLETS

Can be dressed like any of the preceding receipts—with cucumbers is a very favourite dish.

LAMB'S SWEETBREADS in Scollops.

Parboil them for five minutes. Then drain and put them on a plate until cold, slice them in small scollops, fry them with 1 oz. of butter, season with pepper, salt, and the juice of half a lemon. Shake in a tablespoonful of flour and some sliced button mushrooms; add ¼ pint of cream. Simmer gently over the fire for a few minutes, then add two raw yolks of eggs. Mix well and gently.

This is an excellent preparation to put into a Vol au Vent case, and is called à la Toulouse.

N.B.—The Vol au Vent case can be ordered at any confectioner's. This saves trouble, but whatever it is filled with ought to be made at home.

VOL AU VENT OF LOBSTER.

Cut up the flesh of the lobster into small pieces. Heat some lobster sauce, bind it with lobster butter, put the pieces of lobster into the sauce and fill the vol au vent case.

VOL AU VENT OF SHRIMPS OR PRAWNS.

Prepare some shrimp sauce, to which add fresh butter and shrimp butter made in the same way as the lobster butter. Heat the sauce and put in the shrimps, and fill the vol au vent case.

VOL AU VENT OF OYSTERS.

Parboil 2 dozen large oysters, strain them from their liquor, wash, beard, and cut them into 4; put them in a stewpan with 1 oz. butter rolled in flour, a little good cream, the oyster liquor strained and reduced by boiling to one-half, a little cayenne and salt, and a teaspoonful of lemon juice. Stir it over the fire for five minutes, fill the vol au vent case, put the cover on the top, and serve.

VOL AU VENT à la BÉCHAMEL.

Take some hard boiled eggs, cut them into slices about half-an-inch thick. Put them into a saucepan with some Béchamel Maigre. Stir carefully, so as not to break the eggs. Fill the vol au vent case.

BÉCHAMEL MAIGRE.

Cut in very large dice 3 onions, 1 carrot, and 2 whole shalots, put into the saucepan with 6 oz. of butter. Let them brown on the fire for five minutes, then add 6 oz. of flour, with two quarts of milk, some parsley and a little salt. Reduce it on the fire for quarter of an hour, always stirring with the spoon, then pass through the tammy. Cover the Béchamel with a layer of rather thick melted butter.

COQUILLES DE VOLAILLE.

Take some fillets of chicken browned in a little butter, cut into scollops, and then take an equal number of scollops of truffles prepared in a Madeira sauce. Mix them with a little French thickening. Fill the shells, and cover them with bread crumbs, and put in the oven.

BEEF SCOLLOPS.

Take 1½ lb. of very tender rump steak. Cut the meat into very small squares, then put into a stewpan with a tablespoonful of butter, and brown well. Season with pepper and salt; then simmer for an hour, stirring constantly. Serve very hot, with croutons of bread fried in butter.

FILLETS OF BEEF (Filets de Bœuf).

After having trimmed the fillet and carefully removed all skin and gristle, cut it into slices, flatten them lightly, giving them a round shape. Melt some butter in a frying pan, place in it the slices of fillet, and season with pepper and salt, then *sautez* them on a good fire; turn them the moment you see the gravy appear on the surface, and take them off the fire when on touching them with the finger they appear firm. Dress them in a circle on the dish, drain the butter off the frying pan, put in a little gravy to loosen the glaze which is formed at the bottom by the cooking of the fillets, add a spoonful of French thickening, boil it down, and serve with a little lemon juice. Make a maitre d'hotel butter, by adding a little chopped parsley to a small lump of fresh butter. Spread a layer between each fillet, with fried potatoes in the middle. This may also be served with Madeira sauce, by putting a wine-glass of Madeira wine instead of the gravy, as above, with the spoonful of French thickening. To make the dishes called Filets "sautés aux truffles," or "aux champignons," add either the truffles

F

or the mushrooms sautéd in butter to the thickening; and for filets sautés aux Anchois (anchovies) anchovy butter (after which the fillets must not be put on the fire).

BEEFSTEAK à la Milanaise.

Take 1 lb. of beefsteak, and put it, with some rind or fat of bacon, into a stewpan. Put it on the fire, and when of a nice brown take out the bacon; add some finely-chopped onions and shalots, a bunch of thyme and parsley, a few cloves or allspice, a tablespoonful of vinegar or lemon-juice, the same of Hervey sauce and a tea-cupful of good gravy or broth. Season with pepper and salt, and stew till quite tender; then add a little butter, with a large teaspoonful of flour rubbed into it, and let it stew a little longer. Have ready about ½ lb. of maccaroni which has been boiled, being careful that it is not overdone. Put it into the stewpan with the meat, adding more gravy if necessary, and heat all together. Take out the thyme and parsley, and serve the meat with the maccaroni dished round it.

RISSOLE CUTLETS à l'Italienne.

Mix from 2 to 3 oz. of butter with a small quantity of flour. Mix all together, stirring over the fire. Add gradually half a tumbler of milk, and when of the consistency of thickish custard, take it off the fire. Now take any cold meat, chicken or fish, and two hard boiled eggs, and chop all small; put into the made sauce, mix all together. Leave the whole on a floured marble to get cold, then form into cutlets; egg and breadcrumb them and fry a light yellow. Take small bones from a chicken or a hare to make shanks. Run one through each cutlet, and put a frill of paper at the end. Serve with any sauce; the following sauce, with truffles in the centre of the roll, makes an excellent dish.

TRUFFLE SAUCE.

Wash 10 truffles, and cut them into slices about the size of a penny piece. Then put them into a frying pan, with one tablespoonful of minced parsley, one minced shalot, salt and pepper to taste, and 1 oz. butter. Stir them over the fire that they may all be equally done, which will be in about ten minutes, and drain off some of the butter; then add a little more fresh butter, 2 tablespoonsful of good gravy, the juice of half a lemon, and a little cayenne. Stir over the fire until the whole is on the point of boiling, when serve.

QUENELLE OF RABBIT.

Half boil the rabbits, then take off the meat and mince it. Pound well in a mortar and mix into a stiff paste with 1 egg and a little cream. Season with mace and white pepper. Put into a mould, and tie it up in a cloth. Boil for three-quarters of an hour. Then turn it out, and pour over a white sauce. The mould ought to be the shape of a rabbit.

POULET à la Crapandine (Mauritius Receipt).

Cut a chicken into halves, pepper and salt it, then lay it in a flat stewpan with a heavy weight on it. Be careful to turn the chicken very often. Put some butter on the fire, with onions and a little vinegar. When thoroughly melted add the chicken, and fry a nice brown, then pour over some good brown gravy, and serve with fried onions and mushrooms.

CHICKEN CUTLETS.

Remove the white off the breast of a couple of young fowls. Flatten with a chopper that has been previously dipped in water, trim neatly, sprinkle over some salt, dip in egg and bread-crumbs, and fry them in butter to a light golden colour. Pass a nicely-pared chicken bone through each before cooking, to form a shank. Dish them in the same way as mutton cutlets, and serve with either truffle or mushroom sauce.

CHICKEN CUTLETS à la Tartare.

Half boil two chickens, and make the white and short bones of the legs, which must be flattened, into cutlets. Lard and *sauter* them, and serve very hot with the following cold sauce.

SAUCE à la Tartare.

The yolk of one hard boiled egg to be carefully mixed with the yolk of a raw egg, taking care that they are both cold. Make these yolks into a paste by adding seven tablespoonsful of salad oil, drop by drop, and beating them with the American whisk. When quite thick add one tablespoonful Tarragon vinegar and a spoonful of French mustard, half of a very small raw onion chopped into powder, and twice as much parsley with one small saltspoonful of salt. All must be well mixed.

N.B.—Cold chicken can be done in the same way; a very little Cayenne is sometimes added.

BROILED CHICKEN (Breakfast).

To prevent cold chicken which you broil for breakfast from being hard and dry, rub each piece with oil, and bread-crumb them before broiling. Serve with toasted bacon, or with the following sauce.

Take one large spoonful of mustard, into which you work two tablespoonsful of Harvey sauce, a teaspoonful of Chili vinegar, and the same of shalot vinegar, and one tablespoonful of claret. Heat in a silver dish over a lamp and add to the chicken.

BOMBAY CURRY.

Take 4 good sized onions, slice them fine, and fry till brown and crisp. Put in a small saucepan 3 tablespoonsful of stock, 2 tablespoonsful of curry powder, a dessert-spoonful of chutnee, the same of sugar, and some salt, all well mixed together, and let it boil up once. Cut up 3 lbs. of uncooked meat, chicken, rabbit, or fish into square pieces, add a large apple, pared and cut into thin slices, and put all into the pan with the onions. Then pour over the contents of the small saucepan, and fry for half-an-hour more till of a fine rich colour. Be careful to keep stirring all the time to prevent burning. When nearly cooked, add the juice of half-a-lemon and a tablespoonful of Chili vinegar. Serve in a very hot dish, with the rice separate.

This is a very good receipt for prawn curry, substituting shelled prawns for the meat.

N.B.—I can strongly recommend the Curry Powder sold by Mr. Taylor, chemist, Baker Street.

RICE for CURRY.

Wash a cupful of rice, put it into a saucepan with plenty of cold water and a tablespoonful of salt. Let it boil for about twenty minutes, carefully watching it to see when the grains are soft. Strain through a collander, and let the rice dry before the fire for a few minutes, when each grain ought to be separate.

EGG CURRY.

Slice two onions, and fry them in butter. Add a tablespoonful of curry powder. Stew all in a pint of good broth till the onions are quite tender. Mix in half a pint of cream or milk, and thicken with arrow-root or rice flour. Simmer a few minutes, then add six hard boiled eggs cut in slices. Heat thoroughly, but do not allow them to boil.

CHICKEN and TOMATO SAUCE.

Cut the chicken into joints, and let them lie for two hours in an earthen dish in a pickle made with two tablespoonsful of vinegar, with a little salt and pepper. Drain; then soak each piece in lard or dripping, and fry. Dress them in a circle, garnish with fried parsley, and serve with tomato sauce.

CHICKEN à la Josephine.

Cut up the chicken into small pieces, put them into a stewpan with a piece of butter about the size of an egg, and give them a light brown colour, and dredge well with flour, then add finely chopped parsley chives, and a couple of small onions. Let them fry for a few minutes, then add a little gravy (half a teacupful at a time till you have enough sauce), a little pepper and salt, a small bottle of tomato sauce, and a squeeze of lemon juice. If you can get fresh tomatoes so much the better. They must be boiled separately without water, with a very little bit of butter, and, when quite done, pass them through a sieve. Add them to the sauce, letting all stew slowly by the fire for some minutes before serving.

CHICKENS à la Bresilienne.

Cut up the fowl into pieces, and fry them a light brown. Chop up very fine some chives or green onions and parsley. Put them into a stewpan with the fowl, a cup of gravy or broth, two cloves of garlic pounded with an iron spoon, and two or three tablespoonsful of bacon fat. The latter must be made by frying some fat bacon till burnt to a chip, and the juice poured off when quite dark; add salt and pepper to your taste, but **it** is generally made very hot, and in Brazil in red pepper is used. Let the whole stew till quite tender, and serve very hot with rice done as follows:—

Put the rice down in boiling water with some salt, 2 cloves of garlic pounded in the same way as for the flour, some parsley and chives, and let it cook till quite done, then add 2 or 3 tablespoonsful of the bacon fat, and some pepper, and serve very hot. It should be quite soft and moist.

POULET AU RIZ.

Put the fowl in a saucepan with a pint of broth, 2 or 3 onions, 2 cloves, a bunch of parsley and thyme, a teaspoonful of salt, the same of pepper. Let it boil for fifteen minutes, then take out the thyme, parsley, and onions, add $\frac{1}{4}$ lb. of rice, which must be well washed, and let all stew together for half an hour more, stirring the rice all the time to prevent it getting into lumps. Serve the fowl with the rice round it, and pour three tablespoonsful of good gravy very hot over the whole.

POULET AU BLANC.

Put $\frac{1}{4}$ lb of butter into a stewpan with two tablespoonsful of flour. Let the butter melt, then mix into a paste, add one pint of water and a dozen small onions. Put in the fowl with a bunch of parsley, some pepper and salt. Simmer slowly for an hour and a half. Take out the fowl, skin it, and put it back into the stewpan with a dozen mushrooms, and let it stew for half an hour more, till quite done, and serve with the following sauce poured over it :—

Beat up the yolks of 2 eggs in a small saucepan, squeeze in half a lemon, then add some of the gravy in which the fowl has been boiled, and stir well on the fire till the sauce is thick enough, being careful not to let it boil.

CRÈME de VOLAILLE.

Take either 1 lb. of veal or the flesh of a chicken, pound in a mortar, and then pass through a wire sieve; then put a piece of butter, and again pound in a mortar, then add a little thick white sauce, 2 yolks of eggs, pound again. Then once more pass all through a wire sieve, and mix in 2 tablespoonsful of good cream and add the whites of the eggs well whipped; put into a shape, and steam half an hour. If there is a hole in the centre of the shape fill it with truffles, and serve with white sauce.

CHINA CHILO.

Take a pint-basin full of uncooked or underdone meat, cut it into small dice, with carrots, turnips, cauliflower, lettuce, French beans, or any vegetables you have, cut into similar pieces. Put all into a stewpan, with a small piece of butter and a cup of water, seasoning with pepper and salt. Let them stew till quite tender, and serve. Garnish round with a wall of boiled rice.

TIMBALES.

Take $\frac{1}{2}$ lb. Naples macaroni, boil until quite soft, drain on a cloth. Cut the macaroni in pieces half an inch long; well butter a plain mould (or the timbale cases), line with buttered paper, and place the macaroni edgeways (so as to look like honeycomb). Make the following paste :—

Put a quarter of a pint of water, a small piece of butter, and a little salt into a stewpan. When the water boils throw in a tablespoonful of flour, leave it a few minutes, then stir in one egg, and put all on a plate till wanted. Then take 1 lb.

of veal cutlet, cold chicken, or any cold meat, pound in a mortar, add to it half the quantity of the above paste, and a quarter of the quantity of butter, with salt and pepper to taste. Mix all together, and add one whole egg and three yolks; pass through a wire sieve; stir in a quarter pint of white stock or milk. Pour into the moulds, and steam for half-an-hour. The timbales are also good made with rice, strewing cheese through them.

OYSTERS and BACON (Kebobs).

Take about eight nicely pared thin wooden skewers little more than one finger in length. Parboil and beard some oysters, cut some fat bacon the same size as an oyster; then run a skewer first through an oyster, then a bit of bacon, and so on till each skewer is filled. They must then be bread-crumbed, and fried in fat, and sent up very hot nicely piled one on the other.

GERMAN VEAL CUTLETS
(called Wiener Schnitzel).

Cut some slices from a leg of veal about a finger thick. Flatten them with a beater which has been previously wetted. Sprinkle them on each side with salt and pepper; coat them with bread crumbs and white of egg. Fry them in butter till of a bright golden colour, but do not give them too much of the fire, or they will not retain their juice and will be dry. Serve them on a dish, over which pour the butter in which they have been cooked. Put crossways on each slice two narrow strips of anchovies, sprinkling over all some capers without the vinegar, and add slices of lemon.

VEAL SCOLLOPS aux Fines Herbs, or with Sauce Italienne.

Take a piece of fillet about 2½ lbs.,—remove all bone, gristle, and skin.

Cut the veal into equal slices, and flatten them with a beater. Cover the frying dish with a layer of butter, then cover the layer over with salt and pepper.

Range the scollops on the dish close to each other, and dust them also with salt and pepper. Cook them over a sharp fire on both sides for four minutes. Remove the meat and put it on a plate. Put ¼ oz. flour into the frying pan, and stir over the fire for a minute with a wooden spoon. Add three wineglassesful of broth or stock, and boil for five minutes. If any gravy has come from the scollops while on the plate, add it to the sauce.

Dress the scollops in a pyramid (or with the roll in the centre) on the dish they are to be served in. Put the sauce on the fire, and at the first boiling add 1 oz. butter cut into six pieces, and a tablespoonful of minced parsley. Stir with the spoon so as to melt the butter. Pour the sauce on the scollops and serve; or they may be served with Sauce Italienne.

ROGNONS à la Brochette (Kidneys).

Put the kidneys for some minutes in water. Make a small incision on the opposite side of the sinew. Remove the fine skin which is over the kidneys, and split it without separating them. Pass a silver skewer through to prevent them closing during broiling. Put pepper and salt, dip them in oil or clarified butter, and broil them over a quick fire. When done take out the skewers, and put into each kidney some butter the size of a walnut, into which knead some minced parsley and lemon juice. Serve on a hot plate. This is a very nice breakfast dish.

HARE CUTLETS.

(Cotelettes de Lievre—Sauce Groseille.)

Prepare two hares, as if for roasting. Keep the blood. Thrust the knife along the backbone to the leg, and then slipping the fingers between the bones and the fillet, detach the fillet, but without separating from the leg the thick end which holds it. Pass the point of the knife underneath that part, and draw the fillet towards you. When you have thus taken off the four fillets, spread them on the table, and divide each into three parts. Cut them on the bias, so that one end is thick and the other thin.

Flatten them gently, and trim them in the form of cutlets, of which there ought to be twelve. Run a shank through each. Season with pepper and salt. Pass lightly on each a little brush of feathers dipped into the yolk of an egg, breadcrumb them very finely. Soak the cutlets into some very hot clarified butter. Bread-crumb them a second time. Pass the blade of the knife lightly over them to gloss them. Put some butter melted into a stewpan—place the cutlets in and *sautez* them like ordinary cutlets. Put a frill of paper round each cutlet, and dish them as already described, (see page 75), with the following sauce.

SAUCE GROSEILLE.

Dissolve about three teaspoonsful of currant jelly in the same quantity of water, and heat over the fire, adding a little isinglass if necessary.

RABBIT CUTLETS.

Take the back of the rabbits, skin them carefully, and raise the fillets over the bone. Then cut off two pieces the size of a finger from each fillet, and flatten them as for cutlets; run a bone of the rabbit through each to make the shank. Lard each cutlet and fry in butter for barely three minutes, sprinkling them with a little salt while on the fire. Make a gravy with the meat and bones left of the rabbit, adding truffles or mushrooms.

SALMI OF PHEASANT.

Roast a pheasant, taking care not to let it be overdone. When cold, cut into thin pieces and put them in the saucepan. Pound the bones and trimmings, and boil in brown stock for half-an-hour with a few shalots, half a laurel leaf and a pinch of pepper.

Strain through a napkin, skim carefully, and boil the strained broth over a sharp fire for a few moments. Add a little brown thickening and a glass of white wine; keep stirring over the fire till the sauce is of the right consistency, then mix in a pinch of salt, a *very little* sugar, and some lemon, and pour all over the pheasant that has been cut up. Heat the salmi in the *bain marie*, then arrange the pieces neatly in a very hot dish, with the sauce over them. A truffle sauce is a great addition to this most excellent dish.

SALMI OF WILD DUCK.

Proceed in the same manner as for Salmi of Pheasant.

LARDED SWEETBREADS.

Soak for an hour in tepid water to cleanse them. Then whiten in cold water till firm enough to pass a larding-pin through without tearing them.

Wash and drain—press them a little to give them a flat form, and after trimming lard them. Put into the bottom of a saucepan some narrow strips of bacon, on which place the sweetbreads, which are to be cooked with fire above and beneath the saucepan. Done in this manner, they do not require the addition of gravy or broth. Half an hour of the fire is enough for them. Glaze and serve Tomato or any other sauce.

RIZ DE VEAU en Caisses (Sweetbreads).

Oil the paper cases externally, and put at the bottom of each case some stuffing made by the following receipt, then the sweetbread, then cover with more stuffing and some bread crumbs. Bake for a quarter of an hour.

STUFFING.

Mince the following ingredients very fine :—
½ lb. fat bacon, some mushrooms and shalots, add ¼ lb. butter and 4 tablespoonsful of oil. Put on the fire for five minutes; add chopped parsley, then heat again for two minutes, season with pepper, salt, and spice, and lay it aside for use.

N.B.—This stuffing is very useful for cutlets, tongues, &c.

CALF'S LIVER à la Francaise.

Mince the liver, and also four large onions. Put a good bit of butter in the pan, and when melted put in the onions. When they begin to brown add the liver, and fry with the onions, and when done sprinkle over a tablespoonful of flour. Add either a glass of white wine or broth, and a drop of vinegar. Season with pepper and salt, and serve hot. Be very careful to stir the liver well, to allow the sauce to thicken properly. Do not let it boil, and serve as soon as thick enough.

PIGEONS.

Put two or three young pigeons into a saucepan, with a good bit of butter, some onions, and a little gravy or stock. The birds must be nicely browned, then strain the gravy, and serve very hot.

VEGETABLES.

INDEX.

	PAGE
Potatoes à la Maitre d' Hotel,	115
Sieved Potatoes,	115
Potatoe Soufflés,	116
Purèe de Pommes de Terre,	116
Turnips with Cream,	117
Spinach,	117
Cauliflower,	117
Baked Cauliflower,	118
Celery,	118
Asparagus,	119
Salsifis,	119
Scalloped Salsifis,	120
Sorrel with Eggs,	120
Artichokes,	121
Peas,	122
Purèe of Green Peas,	122
Preserved Green Peas,	123
Dried Green Peas,	123
French Beans,	123
French Beans à la Française,	124

VEGETABLES.

POTATOES à la Maitre d'Hotel.

Boil the potatoes and while hot cut them into slices about twice as thick as a shilling. Take a lump of butter about the size of a walnut—put in a stewpan on the fire and when melted dredge in as much flour as will thicken it. Add half-a-pint of good Stock, 2 tablespoonsful of cream, and a little parsley chopped very fine. Season with pepper and salt. Boil up once, and then put in the potatoes. They must not be stirred but merely heated—taking great care not to let them break.

SIEVED POTATOES.

Boil the potatoes carefully, then pass them through a sieve, add salt and a little pepper, and put the dish on which they are to be served into the oven for a few minutes.

POTATO SOUFFLÉS.

Bake some good-sized raw potatoes for an hour and a-half. Scrape out the inside without spoiling the shell. Mix with the potatoes some flour, a bit of butter the size of a nut, a pinch of salt, and as much cream as will make it the consistency of thick cream. Put it into a stew-pan, and boil for a few minutes, stirring all the time with a fork; then fill the potatoe shells with the mixture, heaping it up very high, and be careful to do it loosely, so as to allow the souffles to rise. Put them into a quick oven for ten minutes. Have ready a dish with a napkin on it. Lay them on it, and serve at once, before they fall.

PURÉE de POMMES de TERRE.

Put into a saucepan 2 lbs. of mealy potatoes well washed and peeled, cover with water, add salt, and when nearly three-quarters boiled throw away the water and put them in the oven till sufficiently done. Pass them through a tammy, a small quantity at a time, then put the purée into a saucepan, add a little butter, one or two yolks of eggs, and some cream.

TURNIPS WITH CREAM.

Pare and wash in hot water, then put them on the fire in boiling stock; add a little butter and salt, and boil gently till tender, keeping the saucepan well covered all the time; pour off the broth, and boil again with some flour, mixed with a little butter, a pinch of pepper, some cream, and a very little sugar, and serve very hot.

SPINACH.

Let the spinach be well washed, and soak in cold water till you are ready to cook it. Put it into a saucepan of boiling water, and when done enough drain. Then chop it very fine, and pound it with some butter, previously melted on the fire. Add some cream, and when all has boiled together for a few minutes, serve with bread sippets fried in butter.

CAULIFLOWER.

Trim and clean it well, wash in cold water, put it into a saucepan with boiling water, some butter, and salt, and boil till tender; then drain through a sieve. Serve on a dish with the following sauce:—Beat 6 oz. of butter to cream, mix in the yolks of 3 eggs, and a spoonful of flour. Pour some of the water in which the cauliflower has been boiled gradually into the sauce, constantly stirring while on the fire till of the right consistency. When on the point of boiling take it off the fire, and add a little butter.

BAKED CAULIFLOWER.

After the cauliflower is boiled, let it drain on a napkin. Prepare a thick sauce according to previous receipt, and let it get cool. Arrange the cauliflower on the dish in which it is to be served, cover it with the sauce, scatter over thickly some bread crumbs and grated Parmesan cheese, and bake in a very hot oven, taking the precaution of placing the dish on a baking tin, covered with ashes or salt a finger deep.

CELERY WITH DUTCH SAUCE.

Pare the heads nicely, and cut into lengths, then boil them in salt water till tender. Then drain off all the water, and pour a Dutch sauce over the celery.

ASPARAGUS.

Peel the asparagus smooth and fine, then wash and tie in bundles of ten or fifteen—taking care that the heads are all of the same size—the ends cut even, put them into boiling water slightly salted, and boil over a quick fire. If to be dished immediately, boil till quite tender (from ten to fifteen minutes will be sufficient) but if obliged to boil them some time before wanted it is better to leave them only half the time on the fire, and then in a hot place till sufficiently tender.

Lay the asparagus on a cloth till the water is completely drained off, and then serve with either the same sauce given for cauliflower, melted butter, or Dutch sauce.

SALSIFIS.

This is a vegetable not often met with in England. It is excellent when properly dressed. Take off the skin and scrape till quite white, and then put immediately into cold water. Have boiling water ready in the saucepan, put in the salsifis with some salt, and boil from ¾ to 1 hour, keeping them well covered all the time. Drain and serve with the following sauce :—For a large dish take two tablespoonsful of flour, mix with some milk and ¼ lb. of butter, add salt and pepper, always stirring on the fire. When the sauce is ready, just before serving add the yolk of an egg well beaten up in a bowl, and a little vinegar.

SCALLOPED SALSIFIS.

Boil some Salsifis roots till tender—cut them across into slices. Stew in half-a-pint of good white sauce—with a tablespoonful of anchovy. Put them into shells in layers with breadcrumbs between. Lay small pieces of butter on the top—strew breadcrumbs over the whole, season with pepper and put them in the oven to brown.

SORREL WITH EGGS (Œufs à l'Oseille).

Pick and wash the sorrel, put it in a saucepan on the fire. When the juice is extracted pass through a tammy, add butter, pepper, and salt, and heat again for a few minutes on the fire. Then add some cream, and serve with hard boiled eggs cut in quarters, and piled in the middle and round the dish.

ARTICHOKES.

Cut the tops, stalks, and outer leaves of the artichokes, pare off the green from the bottoms, rub the latter with lemon juice, and throw the artichokes into cold water, then boil them in salt and water till sufficiently tender to allow of the inner leaves being removed. Let the artichokes cool in cold water, take away first the small middle leaves, and then the choke, wash again and put them into a saucepan with a little stock or water, salt, pepper, lemon juice, and butter, and simmer over a gentle fire till tender. The lid of the saucepan must always be kept on. When ready to serve, remove them carefully so that they do not fall to pieces, and place them the wrong side uppermost on a cloth to drain, then dish them. Fill the centre with thick melted butter or Dutch sauce.

PEAS.

The peas ought to be very young. Boil them in very bubbling salt and water for a quarter of an hour, then pass through a collander to drain, and dish them with small lumps of fresh butter.

When the peas are getting older the following is a very good mode of cooking them. Pour over them three or four tablespoonsful of water, add some fresh butter, and simmer over the fire till tender, constantly shaking the pan.

When the peas are soft, mix in some butter and flour, to the proportion of two table spoonsful of butter and half a tablespoonful of flour to two quarts of peas. Shake again over the fire, add chopped parsley, and let them heat but not boil any more. When ready to serve add a little sugar; and some water or broth if too thick; but if too thin a little more butter and flour.

PURÉE OF GREEN PEAS.

Thick green peas are the best for this dish. Boil till tender in broth or water, with a little butter and salt, then pass through a sieve with a bunch of parsley which has been boiled in water, and make into a thick pulp with a lump of fresh butter, some broth, sugar, and a little salt, and stir on the fire till heated through.

PRESERVED GREEN PEAS.

Take a tin of preserved peas ; pour them into a collander to drain off the juice ; then take two tablespoonsful of butter, well mixed with one of flour, add some broth or water, and boil all into a thick sauce, putting in a little salt, sugar, and chopped parsley. Just before serving stir the sauce hot, then put in the peas, and shake the pan over the fire till they are heated through, and serve.

DRIED GREEN PEAS

Steep for twenty-four hours in river or rain water, put on the fire in cold water, and boil till very tender. Pour into a collander to drain, and proceed as in previous receipt for preserved green peas.

FRENCH BEANS.

When young the best way of dressing French beans is to cut them in thin strips, and to boil them in plenty of boiling salt and water till tender. Let them drain on a sieve, then serve them on a dish piled up, with *very small* pieces of butter scattered through them.

FRENCH BEANS á la Francaise.

After the beans have been boiled and drained through a sieve as above, put them into a saucepan with a little butter, salt, and pepper, adding some stock thickened with a little flour, and heat over the fire.

RELEVÉS—(REMOVES).

INDEX.

	PAGE
Saddle of Mutton,	129
Loin of Mutton (boned),	129
Fillet of Beef—Madeira Sauce,	130
Stewed Sirloin of Beef,	131
Veal à la Bourgeoise,	131
Fricandeau of Veal,	132
Purée of Sorrel,	132
Roast Lamb,	133
Saddle of Lamb,	133
Shoulder of Lamb,	133
Boiled Chickens,	133
Boiled Turkey,	134
White Sauce,	134
Mushroom Sauce,	134
Celery Sauce,	135
Chickens with Tarragon Sauce (Poulets à l'Estragon),	135
Roast Chickens	136
Roast Turkey (with Oysters),	136
Bread Sauce,	137
Roast Capon,	137
Roast Ducks, Tarragon Sauce (Canards à l'Estragon),	137
Roast Goose,	137
Chestnut and Apple Sauce,	138
Ham,	138

RELEVÉS—(REMOVES).

SADDLE OF MUTTON.

This is a less expensive dish for a small party than is imagined. The Alderman's Walk being cut out, makes one dish (see Filet Mignon), a roast joint the second, and the following day it can be heated up by placing a piece of buttered paper over it, and roasting it again carefully; and after that the remains can be made into rissole cutlets, the bones being put into the stock pot.

LOIN OF MUTTON (Boned).

Bone a loin of mutton, take off the flap and skin, then flour it and put it into a stewpan, the lean side downwards, with a pint of water, an onion, and a few cloves. Stew it gently for an hour, then turn the mutton, the fat side downwards, and stew it for an hour and a half longer.

Skim the gravy well, and then add a glass of port wine and a teaspoonful of essence of anchovy.

FILLET OF BEEF.

Get a sirloin of beef. To get a good fillet for an end dish it must be pretty large. Cut out the fillet, trim and lard it the night before, and let it lie until the next day in a seasoning of pepper, salt, onions cut into shreds, and parsley in branches. Just before putting to the fire, take away the parsley and onion. Put it on the spit with buttered paper, roast, and five minutes before it is done take off the paper. Serve in its own gravy, garnish with bunches of carrots, turnips, and cauliflowers,—Madeira sauce in a separate boat.

MADEIRA SAUCE.

Put into a saucepan ¾ pint of Madeira, 1¼ oz. of glaze, and a pinch of mignonette pepper. Reduce it to half. Add 1½ pint of French thickening, and continue reducing till the sauce coats the spoon.

STEWED SIRLOIN OF BEEF.

After the fillet has been taken out, carefully remove the bones of the sirloin. Spread it flat on a table; strew over it a little salt and pepper, and then cover the inside with thin slices of striped bacon. Roll and bind up the meat firmly. Lay it in a thick iron saucepan of nearly its size. Add the bones, and as much good beef-broth as will nearly cover the joint. As soon as it has boiled a few minutes, and been well cleaned from scum, throw in a large bunch of savoury herbs, leeks, and one onion, stuck with a dozen cloves. An hour later add two blades of mace and half a dozen peppercorns. Stew the beef very gently from four to five hours, or longer. Serve with brown caper sauce. Add what salt may be needed before the vegetables are thrown in, and after the meat is lifted out the liquor in which it has been stewed will make very good soup.

VEAL,

(à la Bourgeoise).

Take a piece of veal, with some of the kidney fat, or a bit of a fillet. Put it with a little butter in the saucepan on the fire till of a good colour. Then add half-a-pint of water, a bunch of herbs, 2 or 3 onions, pepper, and salt, some carrots (or potatoes which have been half-done), and let it simmer over a slow fire for about three hours; the lid of the saucepan must be kept on, putting fire on the top. Strain and serve.

FRICANDEAU OF VEAL.

Take the centre part of a hind quarter of veal, trim, and remove the skin and gristle, and lard it. Line the bottom of a saucepan with carrots and onions. Add a little gravy or broth, and cook very gently, with fire above and beneath, for three hours, and baste with its own gravy, taking care not to let it brown. Skim and thicken the gravy, and serve with a Purée d'Oseille (Sorrel), spinach, peas, or tomatoes.

N.B.—This may be served either as an end or side dish.

PURÉE OF SORREL (OSEILLE).

Take about two handfuls of sorrel, pick and put it into a saucepan on the fire. When the juice is extracted pass through a tammy;

then add a little butter, pepper, and salt, and heat again for a few minutes on the fire. Before serving add a little cream and the yolks of 2 eggs.

ROAST LAMB.

Take a hindquarter of lamb. Cut off the knuckle-bone, put it on the spit. Roast, dress, garnish with water-cress, and serve with horse-radish sauce.

SADDLE OF LAMB.

Trim a saddle of lamb, and put it on the spit. Roast it, and serve with water-cresses and sauce piquante.

SHOULDER OF LAMB.

This is very good with Tomato sauce.

BOILED CHICKENS.

They must be boiled gently, and in order to have them very white, just as they are on the point of boiling take them out, skim and put them back into the pot. Serve with white celery or mushroom sauce, and slices of lemon.

BOILED TURKEY.

Proceed in same manner and put the usual stuffing.

WHITE SAUCE FOR CHICKENS.

Take about one quart of white stock, put it into a stew-pan with a little parsley, herbs, and a bay leaf. Add a little salt. When it has boiled long enough just to taste of the herbs, strain and boil it up again till reduced nearly one-half. Mix a tablespoonful of arrowroot with a pint of cream, and simmer very gently for five minutes over a slow fire. Add the prepared stock to it, and simmer slowly for ten minutes, if the sauce is thick; but if too thin, stir over a sharp fire till it thickens. It is better to be thick, because it can always be thinned with either cream, milk, or stock.

MUSHROOM SAUCE.

Take $\frac{1}{2}$ pint button mushrooms, cut off the stalks and wipe free from grits. Dip into lemon-juice and water, to whiten them. Chop fine, and put into a saucepan with 1 oz. of butter. When soft add half a pint of white sauce, and simmer till done enough. Rub all through a tammy, and serve very hot.

CELERY SAUCE.

Boil six heads of celery in salt and water till tender, and cut into pieces two inches long. Put one pint of white stock into a stewpan with a few herbs and a little mace, and simmer for half an hour to extract their flavour. Then strain, add the celery, and a thickening of butter kneaded with a little arrowroot. Just before serving put in about ½ pint of cream. Boil up, and add a little lemon-juice.

CHICKENS with TARRAGON LEAVES.
(Poulets à l'Estragon).

Make a white sauce with consommé of chicken, and bind it with the yolks of two or three eggs, adding a good handful of chopped tarragon leaves. Half-boil the chickens, then take them out, and skin them; put them back into the above sauce, and boil till sufficiently done.

N.B.—Tarragon is not much grown in England, which is to be regretted. In foreign countries it is much used in cookery. The roots may be procured from France, and will be found to grow perfectly well in England.

ROAST CHICKENS.

Before roasting, tie on each side of the breast a slice of fat bacon, and put a bit of butter and half an onion inside. Keep basting with butter. Serve with water-cress and bread sauce.

ROAST TURKEY with Oysters.
(American Receipt.)

Prepare the turkey for roasting; then stuff it, leaving plenty of room for the stuffing to swell. Sew up with coarse thread. Then make several cuts in the fleshy part of the bird with a sharp knife. Press a good-sized plump oyster into each cut, as far in as possible. Draw the skin over it tightly, and make it cover each cut. Sprinkle over some flour, pepper and salt, and put a little of each into the dripping-pan, with some water. Baste the turkey constantly with its own drippings. Bake a clear golden brown, taking care not to scorch it.

BREAD SAUCE.

Peel and slice an onion, and simmer in a pint of new milk until tender. Take about a breakfastcupful of stale bread; break it into small pieces into a saucepan. Strain the hot milk over it (having taken the onion out), cover close, and soak for one hour. Then beat up smooth with a fork. Add a very little cayenne, salt, and 1 oz. of butter. Boil and serve.

ROAST CAPON.

To be roasted the same as chicken, and served with bread or egg sauce.

ROAST DUCKS with TARRAGON LEAVES.
(Canards à l'Estragon).

Roast the ducks, (they ought to be rather under- than over- done), and then heat them in the tarragon sauce, the same as for the chickens.

ROAST GOOSE.

Roast as chicken, and serve with chestnut and apple sauce.

CHESTNUT AND APPLE SAUCE.

Peel the chestnuts, throw them into boiling water, let them just come to the boil, then take off the fire, remove the second skin, and wash them. Boil till tender, and then stew them in a little butter and sugar.

Peel and slice some apples, steam in a little water till tender, add some wine, sugar, and lemon-peel, and mix with the chestnuts.

HAM.

Soak the ham for a few hours in vinegar and water. Then put it on the fire with sufficient cold water to cover it, bring it gradually to the boil, and as the scum rises, carefully remove it. Simmer very gently until tender. When it boils add 2 heads of celery, 2 turnips, 3 onions and a large bunch of savoury herbs. When done take the ham out, strip off the skin, cover with bread raspings, and put a frill round the knuckle. If to be eaten cold, the ham must remain in the water till nearly cold. Then remove the skin and glaze it.

RÔTS—ROASTS.

INDEX.

	PAGE
Roast Ducklings—Green Peas (Canetons aux Petits Pois),	143
Turkey Poults—(Dindonneaux),	143
Guinea Fowl—(Pintade),	143
GAME—(Remarks on Roasting),	144
Woodcock—(Bécasse),	144
Snipe—(Bécassine),	145
Wild Duck—(Canard Sauvage),	145
Wild Duck (German Fashion),	145
Partridge—(Perdrix),	145
Grouse,	145
Boiled Pheasant—Cream Sauce—(Faisan Sauce à la Crème),	146
Cumberland Sauce for Game, Cold,	146
„ „ Hot,	146

RÔTS—(ROASTS).

ROAST DUCKLINGS and PEAS

Are usually served with green peas.

TURKEY POULTS and GUINEA FOWL.

Turkey poults and guinea fowl ought to be larded, and a bit of butter, with half an onion, put into the breast, and served with bread sauce.

GAME.

Brown game must be most carefully roasted, rather under- than over- done, especially wild fowl. The too common defect of badly-made toast and indifferent melted butter ruins both the look and the flavour of the birds. For roasting game see that the fire is clear, and the birds kept well basted, floured, and frothed.

The following receipt for cooking game is preferred by many to roasting:—

Put a good sized piece of butter into a saucepan. Put the bird breast downwards in the pan. Put the lid on, and cook for ten minutes, then turn the bird on its back and cook for five minutes; then, if not sufficiently done, turn it on its breast again, and let it cook for another five minutes. Make a piece of crisp toast, pour a little of the butter over it. Place the bird on it, and serve very hot.

WOODCOCK.

Roast them as above, from about fifteen to twenty minutes. Place some slices of toast very crisp and thin in the dripping-pan to catch the trails. Serve with a little gravy, round not over them, and with melted butter in a separate boat.

N.B.—The receipt of an epicure for cooking a woodcock was to keep it a long time, and to remove the trail; and then, when ready to be cooked, to put the trail of a fresh woodcock inside.

SNIPE

Must be done and served in the same way as woodcock, and sent up very hot and expeditiously.

WILD DUCK

Must be roasted and served with slices of lemon, and hot Cumberland sauce.

WILD DUCK (German Fashion).

Prepare the bird as for roasting; rub in some flour, and put it on the fire, with butter on both sides of the breast and back, till brown, and then stew over a moderate fire with a little water, a glass of wine, an onion, some herbs, and a little salt, keeping them constantly basted. Thin the gravy with a little water or broth, sharpen with lemon-juice and add some anchovy butter, and pass through a sieve.

Partridges, Grouse, and Pheasants are generally roasted, and served with bread sauce; but boiled pheasant with cream sauce has the merit of novelty.

BOILED PHEASANT.

Let the pheasant be boiled the same way as a chicken, and serve with cream sauce.

CREAM SAUCE.

Put 2 oz. of butter into a saucepan, dredge in a teaspoonful of flour, and keep shaking round till the butter is melted. Add salt and a very little cayenne, and one-third of a pint of good cream, stirring the whole till it boils. Let it simmer for five minutes, when add a little lemon juice.

CUMBERLAND SAUCE for Game (Cold).

One teaspoonful mustard powder dissolved in a large glass of claret, adding some currant jelly and some chopped orange and lemon peel.

CUMBERLAND SAUCE (Hot).

Drain from all fat some good gravy from roasted meat; add a little stock, a glass of strong wine, some currant jelly, and mustard powder. Then strain through a sieve.

SAVOURY DISHES.

INDEX.

N.B.—Those marked with an asterisk (*) are served after the sweets.

	PAGE
Omelettes,	151
Omelette aux Fines Herbes,	151
Ham Omelette,	152
Omelette aux Rognons,	152
* Cheese Omelette	152
* Soufflé au Fromage,	153
Buttered Eggs,	153
Scotch Woodcock,	153
Anchovy Canapees	154
* Cheese Canapees,	154
Scolloped Eggs—American Receipt,	155
Oysters in Shells,	155
* Macaroni and Cheese,	155
* Bloaters on Toast,	156
Ham Toast,	156
Oyster Toast,	156
* Cheese Straws,	157
* Toasted Cheese,	157
Stewed Prawns,	158
Stewed Lobster,	158
Salad Sauce,	159
Mayonnaise Sauce,	159
Prawn Salad, or Lobster Salad,	160
Winter Salad,	160
Meat Jelly,	160

	PAGE
Aspic Jelly,	161
French Butter,	162
Anchovy Butter,	163
Green Butter,	163
Lobster Butter,	164
* Sardines with Oil,	164

SAVOURY DISHES.

(Generally included in the bill of fare under the heading of "Rôts.")

OMELETTES.

The success of an omelette depends upon the following essentials. First, the eggs must not be beaten for more than one minute; secondly, the pan must not be used for any other purpose; and thirdly, the omelette ought not to be served till the very moment it is required.

OMELETTE aux Fines Herbes.

Break 6 eggs into an earthen pan. Add 5 pinches of salt, 3 of pepper, and half a tablespoonful of minced parsley. Whip them with a fork to break the whites, and to amalgamate them with the yolks, *but only for one minute.*

See that the pan is very clean. Put 3 oz. of butter into it, and put it on a sharp fire. Shake it so that the butter melts, but without being coloured. When it is hot, throw in the eggs, and toss with the fork, so that they are done equally.

When they begin to be set, shake the pan, and turn it. Fold down the two sides of the omelette, so as to give it an oval shape. *Sautez* it lightly to colour it, and then toss it on the dish and serve at once. For a smaller omelette 3 or 4 eggs only may be used.

HAM OMELETTE.

Proceed as in the previous receipt, adding to the beaten eggs ¼ lb. of lean cooked ham cut into small squares, with a little pepper.

OMELETTE aux Rognons.

Sautez three kidneys and place them in the middle of the omelette.

CHEESE OMELETTE.

Prepare the omelette according to the first receipt, but without parsley. Season with a little salt and pepper. Grate 1 oz. Parmesan cheese, and add it to the beaten eggs. Serve very hot, and before turning over the sides of the omelette, scatter over 1 oz. Gruyère cheese.

SOUFFLÉ au Fromage.

Take ¼ lb. grated cheese, add the yolks of 2 eggs well beaten, to which add half a pint of boiling milk, which has been poured on some crumbs of bread (the crumb of a penny roll is best). Before putting in the oven add the whites of 4 eggs, well beaten, and serve immediately.

BUTTERED EGGS.

Melt a small lump of butter in the saucepan, then put in three eggs, well beaten and a little salt. Stir well on the fire. When almost done take off the saucepan, and keep stirring for a few minutes Spread some anchovy paste on hot buttered toast, then lay the buttered eggs on the top.

SCOTCH WOODCOCK.

Split 6 anchovies, bone, wash, and warm before the fire. Mix 2 eggs, with one tablespoonful of cream. Put all into the saucepan and stir continually over the fire until thick, then add a little grated tongue over it.

ANCHOVY CANAPEES.

Take some squares of bread with the crust cut off and fry them in butter a light golden colour, free some anchovies from the bones and clean them well, then take half of them, mince fine, and pass them through a sieve, with the yolks of 4 hard-boiled eggs. Mix into a thick paste with some butter and oil. Add mustard, pepper, chopped parsley, chives, capers, a little tarragon, and plain vinegar. Spread on the toast while it is very hot, and lay on each piece the remainder of the anchovies cut into neat strips.

CHEESE CANAPEES.

Take 4 oz. grated cheese, 2 oz. pounded ham, a large tablespoonful of mixed mustard, a *very little* Cayenne pepper and salt. Mix into a paste with the yolk of an egg, spread it thickly between two thin slices of bread, cut into shapes, and fry for one minute in boiling lard.

SAVOURY DISHES.

SCOLLOPED EGGS—(American Receipt).

Take some fine bread crumbs, pepper, salt, parsley, and some melted butter. Make it into a soft paste with milk, and half fill some scollop-shells with the mixture.

Break one egg carefully upon the top of each, dust with pepper and salt. Set in the oven, and bake for about eight minutes until the eggs are well set.

OYSTERS IN SHELLS.

Parboil the oysters, and put them in the pan, with some fresh butter, finely-chopped herbs, seasoned with a little pepper, and a glassful of white wine. *Sautez* them without boiling; when the sauce is thick, add the yolks of 2 or 3 eggs, and the juice of a lemon.

Put 3 or 4 oysters into each shell, cover with the sauce, bread-crumb, and heat them in the oven for a few minutes.

MACARONI AND CHEESE.

Boil the macaroni in milk, adding more milk as it soaks up. Boil very slowly fully two hours.

Then butter a flat dish, and put in the macaroni. Grate some cheese over it, lay small bits of butter over the cheese, and put it in the oven. Add a rim of pastry round the dish, if liked.

BLOATERS ON TOAST.

Parboil 3 or 4 bloaters just long enough to allow the skin to come off easily. Remove it, and take out the meat in fillets (four to each fish). Have ready some slices of well-buttered toast. Lay a fillet on each, and then trim all to the same size. Rub each fillet over with some butter, a slight dust of cayenne and black pepper, and put them in the oven to get quite hot, then serve.

HAM TOAST.

Take some finely-minced ham, and mix it with sufficient cream to make a thin paste, and boil five minutes. Have ready a well-buttered toast and lay the mixture on it. Then strew some bread crumbs mixed with a little parsley on the top, and brown in the oven.

OYSTER TOAST.

Scald a quart of fresh, large, plump oysters in their own liquor. Then pound them in a mortar till they form a paste. Add a little cream, pepper, and salt if necessary. Have ready some squares of hot toast, on which spread the oyster paste. Heat in the oven, and just before serving sprinkle over some finely-chopped pickles.

CHEESE STRAWS.

Rub $\frac{1}{4}$ lb. of butter into $\frac{1}{2}$ lb. of flour, add $\frac{1}{4}$ lb. grated Parmesan cheese, a teaspoonful of flour of mustard, a saltspoonful of cayenne, and one of salt. Mix all well together, then add the whites of 2 eggs well beaten with $\frac{1}{4}$ pint of cold water, and make into a firm paste. Knead, and then roll it out the eighth of an inch thick, and cut into strips, each about 5 inches long. Bake in a quick oven (for about five minutes) till of a pale brown colour. Pile the straws prettily on a dish and serve hot.

TOASTED CHEESE.

Put 4 oz. of double Gloucester cheese in a saucepan, with two tablespoonsful of cream and two pats of butter. Then put on the fire and stir till boiling; take it off and stir in one well-whisked egg. Put it back on the fire, and continue stirring until just on the *point* of boiling, when pour into a dish and brown it with a salamander. Be very careful that it does *not* boil, or it will curdle.

STEWED PRAWNS.

Put into a stew-pan a heaped tablespoonful of flour and 3½ oz. butter. Blend carefully without heating, add pepper and salt and a glassful of warm water. Put the mixture on the fire and stir it—two minutes will be enough. Then take it off, add the juice of a lemon and 6 oz. butter. Stir till the butter is melted. If the sauce is too thick add water till of the right consistency, and keep hot without boiling. Skin the prawns and put them in the sauce.

N.B.—This preparation is also very good for filling a vol au vent case.

STEWED LOBSTER.

Take the flesh, brain, and coral of the lobster, and put into a saucepan with a good lump of butter, a little vinegar, and cayenne, and heat thoroughly.

N.B.—This is much the best way of dressing hot lobster. Avoid sauces or flavourings.

SALAD SAUCE.

Put the yolks of 4 fresh eggs into a basin, mix in drop by drop one quart bottle of oil, and stir with a wooden spoon till all is worked into a good lump. Add 2 teaspoonsful of salt, 2 teaspoonsful of made mustard, 2 tablespoonsful of Chili and the same of French vinegar, Worcestershire and Harvey sauce. Mix all well. Then add by degrees 1 quart of good cream, and bottle for use. This will keep, if well made, for six months, and is far superior to the preparations sold as salad dressings.

MAYONNAISE SAUCE.

Mix the yolk of one raw egg, and the yolk of a hard-boiled egg well together, add drop by drop 5 or 6 tablespoonsful of oil, 1 tablespoonful of Tarragon vinegar, a little chutney, and 1 spoonful of meat jelly. This proportion is for four people.

PRAWN SALAD.

This is even better than lobster salad.

Make the Mayonnaise as above, which is improved by being placed on ice for an hour before using. Then put in your fish shelled, and garnish the dish with hard-boiled eggs cut in quarters.

WINTER SALAD.

Cut 2 Spanish onions, well boiled, into slices, arrange them neatly in a salad bowl, and just before serving pour over a dressing composed of good cream, vinegar, mustard and salt to taste. Add beetroot which has been boiled two hours —and then cut in slices.

MEAT JELLY FOR ASPIC.

Split 6 fresh calves' feet. After having removed the upper part of the bone, put it on the fire with 3 lbs. of beef and 5 quarts of water. Skim well. Add two onions, some carrots, celery, shalot, 2 laurel leaves, a little pepper. Simmer gently from four to five hours, pass through a sieve, then boil again till reduced to two quarts. Let it get cold and stiffen. Then remove all the fat, adding vinegar, a little white wine, and some fresh tarragon leaves. Then beat up 3 eggs, with a little water and the crushed shells of the eggs. Beat all well together and mix with the jelly, and let it boil up again, constantly whisking it while on the fire. Leave it on the side of the fire without touching it for half-an-hour till the eggs have set. Then let it drain through a cloth back and forwards till quite clear. Keep the aspic in an earthen or china vessel for use.

N.B.—If required to be of a dark colour, add some meat gravy before clearing.

ASPIC JELLY.

Cut out the flesh of a fine lobster into scallops and season with salt, pepper, and lemon juice. Spread on a flat baking-tin a layer of French butter, set it on ice, and when frozen cut out of it, with a paste-cutter, scallops the same size as the lobster scallops. Proceed in the same manner with the lobster butter. Now take a mould and fill the bottom with aspic jelly, decorating it with truffles and the whites of eggs. Then fill up the mould with alternate rounds of lobster and butter in the following order :—

First, a round of lobster scallops, then one of *French* butter, the next a round of lobster scallops, then one of *lobster* butter, the concluding rounds to be scallops of lobster and *lobster* butter (each scallop alternated), and the last round scallops of *lobster* and *French* butter alternated. Each round must be separated by a layer of jelly, and after each layer set the mould on ice, so as to make a firm foundation upon which to lay the next round. Finish by the layer of jelly. When sufficiently iced, turn out of the mould and serve on a base of rice made as follows:—Take some rice, wash, and then boil in salt and water. Cover the saucepan so as to allow the rice to burst, simmer over a gentle fire. Pound the rice and put into a narrow oval mould. When cold turn out, and cover it with French butter to colour it. This is not to be cut, but forms a good base for the jelly.

FRENCH BUTTER.

Take a handful each of chervil, Tarragon, Burnet, chives, and watercresses.

Pick and wash them, scald for two minutes in boiling water, drain and let them cool. Having squeezed them perfectly dry, pound them in a mortar with the yolks of 4 hard-boiled eggs, 2 anchovies well washed, ½ oz. gherkins, and ½ oz. dry capers. Season with pepper and salt, add the smallest quantity of garlic—then pound and pass through a silk sieve.

Clean the mortar well, and put a good lump of butter into it—then add the above, two tablespoonsful of oil, and one of Tarragon vinegar, and mix well.

This butter ought to be of a delicate green colour.

ANCHOVY BUTTER.

Take 6 anchovies, clean and scrape them lightly, take away the bone, pound in a mortar, adding to this paste the same quantity of fresh butter. Then pass all through a hair sieve, and keep by for use.

GREEN BUTTER.

Soak five anchovies in lukewarm water for half-an-hour, then pound them in a mortar very fine. Add half-a-teaspoonful of anchovy paste, and some boiled parsley. Pass all through a wire-sieve to get rid of the bones of the fish, and mix the paste into six pats of butter, adding a very little Cayenne. Serve with cheese.

LOBSTER BUTTER.

Pound the spawn and pass it through a silk sieve, then mix with a little fresh butter. Blend well with a spoon, season with pepper and salt. Heat for one hour in the *bain marie.* Strain through a napkin over a pan of water. Raise the butter which is on the surface of the water, put into a napkin, pass it through the sieve, and then mix with the quantity of butter which you have.

SARDINES, with Oil.

Take them out of their tin cases, wipe them, and serve in a dish with fresh oil over them. Scatter some capers (without the vinegar) over them, and send up brown bread and butter at the same time.

ENTREMETS—(SWEETS).

INDEX.

	PAGE
Riz à l' Imperatrice,	169
Vanille Sugar,	169
Lemon Custard Puddings,	170
Soufflé,	170
Cream Soufflé,	171
Coffee Soufflé,	171
Chocolate Soufflé,	171
Jelly,	172
Rum Jelly,	172
Lemon Jelly,	173
Orange Jelly,	173
Claret Jelly,	174
Timbales au Pain,	174
Sauce for Puddings,	175
Wine Sauce,	175
Custard Pudding,	175
Bread and Butter Pudding,	176
Tapioca Pudding,	176
Rice Pudding,	177
Rice Pudding without Eggs,	177
Albert Pudding,	177
Plum Pudding,	178
Blanc Mange au Citron—(Lemon Blanc Mange),	178
Pudding à la Diplomate,	179
Adelaide Pudding,	179
Clara Pudding,	180
Victoria Pudding,	180

	PAGE
Madelaine Pudding,	181
Madame Angot Pudding,	181
Grape Pudding,	182
Bordeaux Pudding,	182
Soufflé aux Fruits,	182
Guards' Sauce,	183
Crème Brulée,	183
Semolina Blanc Mange,	184
Custard à la Francaise,	184
Chocolate Cream,	185
Bavaroise à la Vanille,	185
Whipped Vanilla Cream,	185
Bavaroise aux Fraises (Strawberries),	186
Charlotte Russe,	186
Italian Cream,	187
Compôte of Oranges,	188
Petits Gateaux à la Vanille,	189
Sweet Omelette,	191
Pommes à la Parisienne,	192
Apples en Robe de Chambre,	193
German Rolls,	194

ENTREMETS—(SWEETS).

RIZ à l' Imperatrice.

Take 2 oz. of rice, put it on the fire with some milk till it splits, taking care not to let it boil too long.

Then put in another saucepan the yolks of 4 eggs, 3 ozs. of sugar, a glassful of milk, and 4 leaves of gelatine. Take it off the fire the instant it is near boiling. Mix the whole together with the rice. When cold add whipped cream. Pour it into a shape, previously decorated with dried fruit (such as cherries, angelica, &c.). Then set on ice.

VANILLE SUGAR.

Vanille sugar is made by filling a small earthen jar with the finest sifted sugar, and sticking into it 3 or 4 pods of Vanilla. Close it up tight, and when you want to have the Vanilla flavouring for anything use this sugar, and then fill it up with more plain sugar. It is much better than the essence.

LEMON CUSTARD PUDDINGS.

Take the yolks of 6, the whites of 3 eggs, the grated rinds of 2 and the juice of 1 lemon, 4 oz. powdered sugar, 2 Naples biscuits grated, and 1 small glassful of brandy. Beat all well together. Add 2 oz. fresh butter and 1 pint good cream.

Butter small moulds, put in the mixture, and bake half an hour in a quick oven.

SOUFFLÉ.

Take 2 tablespoonsful of ground rice, half-a-pint of milk or cream, the rind of a lemon pared very thin, and a bay leaf. Sweeten with Vanille sugar, and let all boil together for ten minutes. Take out the lemon peel and let it stand till cold, then add the yolks of 4 eggs well beaten with sifted sugar. Beat the whites of the eggs separately to a fine froth, and add to the above ingredients. Stir all gently together, then put into a mould, and bake in a quick oven for twenty minutes.

CREAM SOUFFLÉ.

Take 3 yolks of eggs, 3 spoonsful of flour, 1 spoonful of Maraschino, or any liqueur. Mix together and add 1 pint cream. Beat up 4 whites of eggs to a strong froth, and stir them in. Bake in a soufflé tin, and serve very hot in the same dish.

COFFEE SOUFFLÉ.

Take 4 eggs, put the yolks in one basin and the whites in another. Add $\frac{1}{4}$ lb. white sugar to the yolks, and beat both together for twenty minutes, then add a dessertspoonful of the strongest made coffee. Froth the whites of the eggs very stiff, and then add them very lightly to the yolks. Unless mixed very carefully the soufflé will fall. Then pour the whole into a soufflé tin, and put into a very hot oven for five minutes, and serve immediately.

CHOCOLATE SOUFFLE.

Proceed as above, adding to the eggs one dessertspoonful of the best chocolate, grated, instead of the coffee.

JELLY.

Take 4 oz. gelatine, 10 oz. sugar, ¼ pint brandy, ¼ pint best rum, the juice of 6 lemons, and the peel of 3, 12 cloves, cinnamon, and half a nutmeg grated. Add 1 pint of water, and 4 whites of eggs, well whisked together. Whisk the jelly on the fire till it boils, and then allow it to stand by the side with the lid on, (containing live embers of charcoal), for about ¼ an hour. Pour several times through a jelly bag. Set in a mould on rough ice.

RUM JELLY.

Dissolve 2 oz. isinglass, then melt about 6 oz. sugar in a pint of water, adding ¼ pint of rum. Take the whites and shells of 3 eggs, whisk them in a saucepan, and add the isinglass, rum, and sugar. Place this preparation on the fire, and stir with a fork till near boiling. Cover immediately, putting fire above and beneath, and much fire on the lid. When the egg has formed a crust, squeeze in the juice of 2 lemons, and cover again for ¼ an hour. Then pass the jelly through a napkin. It ought to be perfectly clear. Pour into a mould, and set on ice.

LEMON JELLY.

Soak 1 oz. of gelatine in half a pint of cold water. Pour a pint of boiling water over the rinds of 3 large lemons, pared very thin, and cover them with a plate for about ten minutes, leaving them in a place where they will keep hot. Put into a stewpan first the gelatine, then the soaked rinds and the juice of the lemons, and lastly the yolks of five eggs. Stir well over the fire till it begins to thicken like a custard, taking care not to let it boil, or it will curdle. Strain through a piece of muslin, and pour into a mould.

ORANGE JELLY.

Squeeze the juice of 1 Seville and 12 China oranges, to which add the juice and grated peel of a lemon and half the peel of the Seville orange. Dissolve 2 oz. of isinglass in 2 pints of water, and reduce to half. Clarify ½ lb. of sugar, and when the syrup is clear put in the isinglass while the syrup is hot. Boil them well together. Then strain and let it stand till nearly cold, when add the juice and grated rinds. Keep stirring to prevent the peel sinking to the bottom as the jelly stiffens. Then put it into a mould and leave it till next day.

CLARET JELLY.

Put into a saucepan a bottle of claret, 8 oz. of lump sugar, the peel and juice of a lemon, a small pot of red currant jelly, and $1\frac{1}{4}$ oz. of isinglass or gelatine dissolved in a little water. Simmer for a few minutes, then boil up once; add half a glass of brandy, strain through muslin into a mould. When cold turn it out carefully, and serve with Vanilla whipped cream placed all round the jelly.

TIMBALES AU PAIN.

Boil 1 pint of new milk, and pour it on half a pound of very finely grated bread crumbs, and let them soak for an hour.

Beat up the yolks and whites of 4 eggs, first separately, then together; and then mix them gradually and thoroughly with the bread crumbs.

When this is done add a little sugar, a teaspoonful of finely-grated lemon peel, 2 oz. butter, broken, ½ a wineglassful of brandy, and stir the whole well together. Then butter the timbale cases and bake them in a moderate oven for about twenty minutes or half-an-hour. When done turn out, and serve with any of the following sauces:—

SAUCE FOR PUDDINGS.

Half a pint of melted butter. Sweeten with white sugar. Stir in a glass of sherry and two tablespoonsful of curaçoa or brandy.

WINE SAUCE.

Mix well together a little fresh butter, a spoonful of flour, some grated lemon peel, and the yolks of 3 eggs. Add about half a tumbler of sherry or Madeira, sweeten with pounded sugar, and stir well while on the fire. The juice of a lemon may also be added.

CUSTARD PUDDING.

Take a spoonful of pounded sugar, and let it dissolve in a plain tin mould, turn it about on the range until it begins to colour, taking care that every part of the mould is covered with it. Boil 1 pint milk with the peel of half a lemon for five minutes, and while boiling pour on 4 eggs lightly beaten. Sweeten and pour into the mould, and put in a stew-pan with enough water to reach half-way up. It must never boil. It will be set in half an hour. Serve with stewed cherries round. (The bottled ones do very well with a little currant jelly added to the sauce.)

BREAD AND BUTTER PUDDING.

Put into a deep dish that will hold a quart, very thin slices of bread and butter (buttered on each side), only half filling it. Strew currants over it, and pour a little brandy over the bread before the custard is added. Stir into a pint and a half of cold milk, 4 teaspoonsful of vanille sugar, and the same of pounded sugar, and 3 eggs well beaten. Then pour this custard into the dish over the bread and butter, and bake in a quick oven.

TAPIOCA PUDDING.

Soak 1½ oz. tapioca in cold water until soft, stirring it now and then. Mix 3 well-beaten eggs with a little vanille sugar and 1 pint cold milk. Stir in the tapioca, and pour the whole into a buttered dish, and bake in a moderate oven.

RICE PUDDING.

Beat 3 eggs very lightly. Stir a little salt, 1 wineglassful of rice, well washed with a little sauce into one quart of milk. Add 2 tablespoonsful of sugar, and 1 tablespoonful butter. Bake one hour in a quick oven.

RICE PUDDING without Eggs.

Take 2 tablespoonsful of rice, one of sugar, and one quart of milk. Flavour to taste, mix all well together, then put into a pie-dish and bake in the oven for two or three hours.

ALBERT PUDDING.

Beat up 4 eggs, leaving out the white of one. Boil ½ lb. of butter in a teacupful of milk. Pour it boiling on the eggs (if preferred you can put ¼ lb. butter and ¼ lb. of fine beef suet), stirring all the time—then add ½ lb. fine bread crumbs, a dessertspoonful of flour, 3 oz. sugar, all well mixed together. Put into a mould decorated with raisins. Steam for three hours.

PLUM PUDDING.

Mix into a fine batter the yolks of 8 eggs, the whites of 4, well beaten with ½ pint of milk, and 1 lb. of flour, add 1 lb. of raisins, 1 lb. of currants, well washed and dried, 1 lb. beef suet, and not cut too small. When all these ingredients are well mixed together add ½ pint milk and ¼ oz. of powdered ginger, and boil six hours.

LEMON BLANC MANGE.

Put a pint of new milk on the fire, and when it boils take it off. Have ready the yolks of 6 eggs, and 2 oz. loaf sugar well beaten, whip them in the milk, and then set it on the fire again, but do not let it boil. Then whip it till nearly cold, add ½ oz. isinglass well dissolved, and whip again till thick. Oil a mould, fill it with the custard, and let it stand till next day. Then turn it out and pour over it the following sauce :—

Make a thin syrup with loaf sugar. Cut the peel of a lemon into very fine chips. When the sugar is boiling, squeeze in some lemon-juice, and when lukewarm throw in the chips. As soon as it is quite cold pour it over the custard before it is sent to table. Ice (if not stiff enough) and serve.

PUDDING à la Diplomate.

Take 8 yolks of eggs, 4 oz. white sugar, ½ pint milk, 5 leaves gelatine. Put them on the fire taking care not to let them boil. Decorate a mould with some dried fruits. Then cut some Naples biscuits the length of the mould. Soak some raisins the night before in white wine, and put a row of cake and a row of raisins alternately. Then pour the mixture over it, and set on ice. Serve with a sauce as for blanc mange, adding white Curaçoa to it.

ADELAIDE PUDDING.

Take 2 eggs, their weight in flour, some fresh butter, and some moist sugar. Beat the yolks and whites separately. Then mix all the ingredients together, adding the whites of the eggs the last. Then add a teaspoonful (not piled up) of Borwick's baking powder, and a teaspoonful of orange marmalade. Pour into a mould or basin, put it into boiling water, boil fast for an hour, and serve immediately with wine sauce.

CLARA PUDDING.

Beat up 3 eggs leaving out two of the whites, add very gradually 1 pint and a-half of milk, 3 tablespoonsful of fine wheaten flour, carefully mixed, 2 oz. finely powdered loaf-sugar, and some grated lemon peel. Boil these ingredients over a slow fire, keep constantly stirring till the flour is well mixed in. Lay some ratifia cakes at the bottom of a shallow dish, pour over them the above mixture, and when cold serve.

VICTORIA PUDDING.

Take 3 eggs, their weight in sugar and butter, and the weight of 2 in flour. Melt and beat the butter to a cream. Beat also the eggs, and add them to the butter and sugar, beating the whole to a froth. Then add the flour by degrees, and the rind of a lemon chopped very fine. Beat all together, pour into a mould, boil gently for one hour, and serve with any sauce preferred. This pudding requires as much beating as a sponge-cake.

MADELAINE PUDDING.

Butter the inside of a plain mould, decorate it with citron and line it with figs. Make a custard with the yolks of six eggs and half-a-pint of cream, sweeten to taste. Pour into the mould and steam for an hour. Let it get quite cold, and serve with wine or brandy sauce, or with custard flavoured with brandy.

MADAME ANGOT PUDDING.

Take $\frac{1}{2}$ lb. finely-chopped beef suet, $\frac{1}{2}$ lb. bread crumbs, the yolks of 6 eggs, $\frac{1}{2}$ pot apricot jam, all to be well mixed together with 1 glassful of sherry. Sweeten to taste. Beat the whites of the eggs to snow, and mix them gently with the other ingredients before putting into the mould, and steam for four hours.

GRAPE PUDDING (German Receipt).

Soak ¾ lb. of crumb of bread in some cold milk, then squeeze it out. Beat ¼ lb. fresh butter to cream and mix with it the following ingredients: the yolks of 8 eggs, ¼ lb. finely pounded sweet almonds, a little lemon peel, and the bread that was soaked in milk. Sweeten with sifted sugar well, and add lastly a soup plate full of grapes with the skins and pips taken off. Mix in gently the grapes, and the whites of the eggs beaten to snow. Boil the pudding in a greased mould for two hours, and serve with wine sauce.

BORDEAUX PUDDING.

Take a bottle of light claret, sweeten and spice as if for mulled wine. When heated, take off the fire and add as much dissolved gelatine as will stiffen it. Pour into a mould, and when cold, turn it out and serve with a rich custard round it.

SOUFFLÉ AUX FRUITS.

Put layers of peaches, apricots, or other fruits (any preserved fruits answer very well), in the soufflé dish. Beat up to a stiff froth the whites of 4 eggs, add ½ lb. of pounded sugar (which must be passed through muslin), put this over the fruit, and bake for two hours.

GUARDS' SAUCE.

Take a good lump of fresh butter. Beat it up to a cream till it appears quite white at night. Add white sugar, and about ¾ glassful of brandy. It ought to look like cream. This is a delicious sauce for puddings, apple tarts, &c.

CRÈME BRÛLÉE.

Put into a saucepan 4 oz. of white sugar with a few spoonsful of water. Put it on the fire, but take it off before the sugar gets too dark a colour. When cold, pour into the saucepan 1¾ pint of milk, and replace on the fire to dissolve the sugar, and when both are well mixed together, add the whipped yolks and whites of 8 eggs. Pass all through a moderately fine strainer. Wipe the saucepan. Pour in again the mixture and place it on a gentle fire, constantly stirring with a wooden spoon. When the cream is thick enough take it off the fire—strain again, and then pour into a mould.

SEMOLINA BLANC MANGE.

Boil 1½ pint of new milk. Sweeten slightly. Stir in 2½ oz. Semolina, and boil eight minutes. Pour into a mould, when cold turn out and serve with cream.

CUSTARD à la Francaise.

Soak 6 dessertspoonsful of tapioca in 1 pint of cold water for five hours. Boil 1 quart of milk, and as it comes to the boil add the tapioca, the water in which it was boiled, and a good pinch of salt. Stir until boiling hot — add gradually the beaten yolks of 3 eggs and some sugar. Boil again, stirring constantly. Let it boil until thick, but not too long. Pour into a bowl, and stir gently into the mixture the whites of the eggs, beaten to a stiff froth.

Flavour, and set aside in a glass dish till very cold. This custard ought to be made in the *bain marie*.

CHOCOLATE CREAM.

1 pint milk, 1 wineglassful of cream, 2 yolks of eggs, half a teacupful of lump sugar, 2 bars Vanille chocolate, not quite 1 oz. of gelatine (as it must not be too stiff). First steep the gelatine in ½ pint of milk for half an hour. Add the sugar and chocolate (grated) to the other ½ pint of milk, boil well, and add to them the eggs well beaten up. Then add the steeped gelatine and milk, beat all together as smooth as possible, and when tepid put into a mould.

WHIPPED VANILLA CREAM.

Dry a pod of vanilla, then pound it with 8 oz. of sugar to powder, pass it through a fine sieve, and mix it with a quart of stiffly-whipped cream. Half of each ingredient may be taken when a smaller quantity is required.

BAVAROISE à la VANILLE.

Boil a pint of cream with a pod of vanilla in it, let it be covered and get cold. Then stir in 2 eggs and the yolks of 4 with some crushed sugar, pour in the cream passed through a sieve and stir over a slow fire till it thickens, being very careful not to let it curdle. Set immediately on ice, and when cool, add 2 or 3 oz. dissolved gelatine. Stir on the ice till it begins to thicken again, then take it off and stir in quickly and lightly 1 pint firmly-whipped cream. Pour into the mould and set it to freeze. Then dip for one instant in warm water, and turn out.

BAVAROISE OF STRAWBERRIES (aux Fraises).

Proceed as for the last receipt, adding with the first cream the strained juice of strawberries. They must be passed through a sieve and the sugar added to the juice. If you find the colour not bright enough, add a little cochineal.

CHARLOTTE RUSSE.

Take a plain copper mould and cover both the bottom and sides very thickly with Naples biscuits, the smooth side being turned outside; then fill it with the Bavaroise, let it get stiff, and turn out on a dish.

ITALIAN CREAM.

Put into a basin half a gill of white wine, a little brandy, two tablespoonsful of pounded sugar, and one of lemon juice. Add 1 pint of cream, and whip all well together. Pour into a shape through a bit of thin muslin. Leave it in a cool place, and before turning out of the mould drain off the whey.

SWISS CREAM.

Heat a pint of new milk very slowly over the fire with the rind of a lemon. Add $\frac{3}{4}$ of an oz. of isinglass and a teacupful of good cream. Let it boil up. Take off the fire and strain. When cool add the well-beaten yolks of 3 eggs and some sugar. Stir well over a slow fire until it begins to thicken, when nearly cold add 1 oz. of almonds blanched and split, 2 oz. preserved ginger cut into small pieces, and pour into a mould.

NORMANDY PIPPINS.

Put 1 lb. of Normandy pippins, with $\frac{1}{4}$ lb. loaf sugar, into a quart of clear spring water, and let the fruit soak all night. Then stew very gently for two hours till of a light brown colour. When cold keep them covered with their own syrup. Be careful not to stew them too long.

STEWED PEACHES.

Take a bottle of preserved peaches and make a clear syrup of the juice with a tablespoonful and a half of sugar. Add a few drops of essence of bitter almonds, and pour the syrup over the peaches.

COMPÔTE OF ORANGES.

Cut each orange into six pieces. Cut off the rinds and core. Put the pieces of orange into a dish with about 1 oz. powdered sugar, and enough warm water to dissolve it. Squeeze the juice out of the rinds into it also. Then cut out all the white parts and cut them into thin chips. Boil till tender. Strain off the water, and mix equal quantities of it and the juice of the oranges, and 2 oz. sugar. Boil till it becomes a thick syrup.

PETITS GATEAUX à la Vanille.

Take the weight of 2 eggs in the shell in butter, flour, and Vanille sugar. Half melt the butter, beat the yolks and whites of the eggs separately, mix the butter and sugar together, then the eggs, and the peel of half a lemon grated, then stir in the flour. Butter the timbale cases—fill them rather more than half full. Bake them in a moderate oven for twenty minutes or half an hour. Serve with the Compôte of Oranges.

LEMON PUDDING à la Lyonnaise.

Put the following ingredients into a saucepan: yolks of 9 eggs, $\frac{1}{2}$ lb. of butter, $\frac{1}{4}$ lb. of finely-sifted sugar, and the juice of a large lemon. Stir all over a gentle fire till it becomes a thick mass, put into a bowl, mix in the rind of one lemon upon which some sugar has been rubbed, and stir till cold and very light. Then add the whites of 10 eggs beaten to snow, and fill a buttered mould, laying a sheet of paper at the bottom. Bake in the *bain marie* in the oven for about an hour and a half. Turn out on a dish, and serve with wine sauce.

GERMAN CABINET PUDDING.

Fill a buttered mould with alternate layers of Naples biscuits, picked Sultana raisins, currants, candied orange and lemon peel cut into dice, preserved cherries, and crushed macaroons. Boil one quart of cream with half a pod of vanilla till the flavour of the latter is extracted. When cool add sugar to taste, a pinch of salt, 2 whole eggs, and the yolks of eight more. Mix all well together, pass through a sieve, and pour gradually over the biscuits and the other ingredients. Then set the mould in a pan of boiling water, cover it, and let the pudding stand either in a moderately hot oven or in a hot place till it is perfectly firm throughout; but taking the greatest precaution never to allow it to boil. Turn it out carefully on a dish, and serve with wine sauce.

ALEXANDRA PUDDING.

Put ½ lb. of bread crumbs into a basin with 2 oz. sago, 6 oz. suet finely chopped, 5 oz. sugar,

4 oz. Sultana raisins, 6 eggs well beaten, half a gill of brandy, and a tablespoonful of rum. Decorate the bottom of a well-buttered mould with green angelica, sultana raisins, candied peel, almonds, ginger, or any dried fruit. Then pour in the mixture, and put the mould into a saucepan of boiling water (which must just cover the half of the mould). Boil gently for two hours over a slow fire; then take it out carefully, and serve with wine sauce.

SWEET OMELETTE.

Take 3 or 4 eggs, mix them with a tablespoonful of milk and a little salt till very clear. Heat 2 or 3 oz. of butter in the pan, then pour in the egg mixture and do the omelet over a pretty sharp fire till the side near the pan is of a light brown colour. Now slip the omelet from the pan on to a sheet of paper and cover the other uncoloured side with apricot, raspberry, or any kind of jam; roll the omelet together, lay it on a dish, sprinkle over some powdered sugar, pass the salamander across the top, and serve very hot.

POMMES à la Parisienne.

Scald 6 fine apples, peel them, and cut into quarters, and rub them with lemon. Boil 2 oz. of rice in some milk. When the rice is dry add the yolks of 3 eggs, turn into a mould, which must have a very narrow rim and on this base of rice place the apples, and decorate them nicely with any kind of dried fruit. Boil down the juice of the apples with some preserved apricot, a little white wine, and a glass of kirsch. When about to serve pour this very hot over the apples, with some crushed macaroons scattered over them.

GERMAN APPLE CHARLOTTE.

Cut the crust of a crisp fresh roll into thin slices. Cut some of the slices with a paste cutter into round pieces the size of a shilling, and the remainder into pieces a finger in length and two in breadth, squaring the ends. Then take a round copper shape, and spread clarified butter all over it, and having dipped each of the round pieces of crust first in clarified butter, then in sugar, lay them at the bottom of the mould and then the long pieces on the sides, taking care that the edges lap over each other so that no space is left between. Pare some apples, cut them in quarters, remove the pips, cut them in slices, and stew them with sugar, a little fresh butter, lemon peel, and two tablespoonsful of rum till half tender; leave them to drain on a sieve and boil the strained juice with some apricot jam, keeping it constantly stirred; then mix in the apples with it, and let all get cold; then fill the shape and cover it with slices of the bread dipped in clarified butter and bake in a moderate oven for about an hour, and immediately after turn out and serve very hot.

If preferred, instead of dipping the bread in sugar, strew some pounded sugar over the Charlotte after it leaves the oven, and pass the salamander over it.

APPLES EN ROBE DE CHAMBRE.

Take some small apples, pare and scoop them out, filling them with sugar, the juice and peel of a lemon, and a little cinnamon. Pour over a glass of rum and let it soak in well for three or four hours before cooking.

Make some paste with butter and cut into pieces large enough each to hold an apple; then lay each piece on a baking tin upon the side where the paste is folded up. Cover with a thin coating of white of egg and sugar; sprinkle with water and bake in a quick oven.

ROAST APPLES.

Scoop out the centre (removing all the pips) and fill it up with butter, cloves, brown sugar, and lemon peel; then roast them. They are also very nice served on croutons of bread fried in butter.

APPLES IN SYRUP.

Peel and cut the apples in quarters, taking out the core. Make a syrup of white sugar, cinnamon, cloves, and spice, and pour over the apples while hot. Let it stand till cold, then heat the syrup again, and pour it boiling hot over the cold apples. Let them stand till the syrup is cold and thick.

GERMAN ROLLS ("Milchbrod").

Stir half a pound of flour with four ounces of yeast and a little tepid milk into a soft mass.

Then take 1½ lb. of flour, and a pint of milk with a little salt, and knead into a soft paste; mix it with the above yeast and flour, and 4 oz. butter, and work the paste very clear; form into rolls, lay them on a baking sheet, let them rise, spread over some egg (previously stirred clear with water), and bake in a moderate oven.

AMERICAN BISCUITS.

Take two large cups of flour, a teaspoonful of yeast powder, the same of salt. Mix well, rubbing in a lump of butter the size of an egg, and make into a paste with a little milk. Roll out once (¾ of an inch thick). Bake for ten or fourteen minutes on a buttered baking-tin in a quick oven. They will rise ¼ of an inch.

COOKIES, or SWEET BISCUITS.
(American Receipt).

Take two cups of flour, one of butter, one of sugar, and one of milk. Mix into a paste. Roll out once (¼ of an inch thick). Bake ten minutes in a quick oven.

SEVILLE ORANGE BISCUITS.

Take 6 Seville oranges, boil them gently in soft water till tender (changing the water several times), then cut them in halves, and take out all the insides, (the outside skin is only to be used). Take twice their weight of sugar finely pounded. Pound the peel and sugar together into a smooth paste. Spread it very thin on sheets of writing paper and let it stand till the following day, then cut the paste into any shapes you like with a tin cutter. Turn them on another dish with a thin knife, and let them dry near the fire for three days.

BOTTLED GOOSEBERRIES.

Put the gooseberries into bottles the moment they are picked, leaving on both the bud at the top and the stalk. Cork closely. Wrap the bottles in hay, and put them in a pot of cold water, on the fire. When it boils take it off, but leave the bottles in the pot till the water cools, then bury the bottles in the ground or keep them in a cool place.

N.B.—This is an excellent receipt.

BOTTLED DAMSONS.

To every lb. of fruit put ½ lb. of loaf sugar. Boil for five minutes and then pour and while very hot into large glass bottles. While filling let each bottle stand in warm water (to avoid cracking the glass). Be careful to fill the bottles well. When cold the fruit will sink down, then cover it with salad oil, which will exclude the air. The mouth of the bottle must be covered with paper to keep out the dust..

INDEX.

Adelaide Pudding, 179
Alexandra Pudding, 190
Albert Pudding, 177
American Biscuits, 195
Anchovy Butter, 163
—— Canapees, 154
—— Sauce, 57
——————, rich, 57
Apples à la Parisienne, 192
—— Roast, 194
—— en robe de chambre, 193
—— in Syrup, 194
Apple Charlotte, 192
Artichokes, 121
Aspic Jelly, 161
Asparagus, 119

Bacon, to prepare for larding, 17
Barley Soup, German, 46
Baked Cauliflower, 118
Bavaroise, Vanille, 185
—— Strawberries, 186
Beans, French, 123
Bechamel, hard eggs, 87
Beef, Fillet of, Madeira sauce, 130
—— Fillets of, larded, 130
—— Scollops, 88
—— Steaks, à la Milanaise, 90
—— Sirloin, stewed, 131
—— Tea, 43
Blanc mange, lemon, 178
—— Semolina, 184
Bloaters on Toast, 156

Bombay Curry, 94
Bonne Femme, Soup à la, 38
Boned Loin of Mutton, 129
Bordeaux Pudding, 182
Bottled Damsons, 197
Bottled Gooseberries, 196
Bread Sauce, 137
—— and Butter Pudding, 176
Brill, 58
Boiled Chicken, 133
Bouillon à la Minute, 37
Bouilli and Soup, 38
Broiled Chicken, 94
Brown Stock, 30
Butter, Anchovy, 163
—— Green, 163
—— Lobster, 164
—— French, 162
Butter Sauce, 53
Buttered Eggs, 153

Capon, Roast, 137
Canapees, Anchovies, 154
Cauliflower, 117
—— Baked, 118
Calf's Liver, 108
Celery, 118
—— Sauce, 135
Charlotte, Apple, 192
—— Russe, 186
Cheese, Canapees, 154
—— and Maccaroni, 155
—— Omelette, 152

INDEX.

Cheese, Soufflé, 153
—— Toasted, 157
Chestnut and Apple Sauce, 138
Chickens, Roast, 136
—— Tarragon Sauce, 135
—— Boiled, 133
—— Mushroom Sauce, 134
—— Brésilienne, 97
—— au Blanc, 98
—— a la Josephine, 96
—— Tomatoes, 96
—— and Rice, 98
—— a la Crapandine, 92
Chicken, Broiled, 94
—— Cutlets, 93
—— Tartar Sauce, 93
Chino Chilo, 100
Chocolate Soufflé, 171
Coffee Soufflé, 171
Claret Jelly, 174
Clear Turtle Soup, 36
—— Hare, 42
—— Ox Tail Soup, 44
—— Julienne Soup, 40
Colbert Soup, 42
Compote Oranges, 188
—— Consommé, 35
—— Chicken, 36
—— Cookies, 195
Crème de la Volaille, 99
Coquilles de Volaille, 88
Crème Brulée, 183
Cream Chocolate, 185
—— Sauce, 146
—— Soufflé, 171
—— Italian, 187
—— Whipped, 185
Cressy Soup, 47
Cumberland Sauce, Hot, 146
—— ——, Cold, 146
Curry, Bombay, 94
—— Egg, 96
Custard Pudding, 175
—— a la Francaise, 184

Custard Puddings, lemon, 170
Cutlets, Chicken, 93
—— Tartar Sauce, 93
—— Hare, 104
—— Rabbit, 105
—— Rissole, 91
—— ——, Truffle Sauce, 91
—— Veal, German, 101
—— Lamb, with Peas, 85
—— with Cucumbers, 86
—— Mutton, plain, with Fried Potatoes, 76
—— Sauce Italienne, 77
—— aux Coucombres, 77
—— a la Maintenon, 78
—— a la Reforme, 78
—— a la Soubise, 79
—— aux Marrons, 80

Diplomate Pudding, 179
Dried Green Peas, 123
Ducks, Roast, 137
—— Roast, Wild, 145
—— —— German fashion, 145
—— Salmi of Wild, 106
Ducklings, Roast, and Peas, 103
Dutch Sauce, 58

Egg Sauce, 57
Eggs, Buttered, 153
Egg, Curry, 96
Eggs with Sorrel, 120
—— Scolloped, 155

Francaise, Soup a la, 37
French Vegetable Soup, 41
—— Onion Soup, 46
—— Melted Butter, 162
—— Thickening for Sauce, 83
—— Mode of Frying Fish, 55
—— Beans, 123
—— a la Francaise, 124
—— Butter, 162
Filet of Beef, 89

INDEX.

Filets of Beef, larded, 130
—— Mignons, 81
—— ——, larded, 82
—— of Soles, boiled, 64
—— —— à la Horley, 65
—— —— and Anchovies, 66
—— of Mackerel, 66
Fish with Curry Powder, 62
Fricandeau of Veal, 132

GAME, remarks on Roasting, 144
Gateaux à la Vanille, 189
German Rolls, 194
—— Veal Cutlets, 101
—— Barley Soup, 46
—— Cabinet Pudding, 190
Goose, Roast, 137
Gooseberries, Bottled, 196
Gravy, 14
Grape Pudding, 182
Gratin, Brillau, 61
Green Peas, Preserved, 123
—— Dried, 123
——, Purée, 122
Grouse, 145
Groseille Sauce, 105
Guinea Fowl, 143
Guards' Sauce, 183

HADDOCK, Boiled, 56
Ham, 138
—— Omelette, 152
—— Toast, 156
Hare Cutlets, 104
—— Soup, 42
Haricot of Mutton, 81
Herrings, Mustard Sauce, 67
Horseradish Sauce, 63

ITALIAN Cream, 187

JELLY, 172
—— Aspic, 161
—— Claret, 174

Jelly, Lemon, 173
—— Meat, 160
—— Orange, 173
—— Rum, 172
Julienne Soup, 40
—— ——, clear, 40

KEBOBS, 101
—— Kedgeree, 62
—— Kidneys, 103

LAMB, Roast, 133
—— Saddle of, 133
—— Shoulder of, 133
—— Sweetbreads in Scollops, 85
—— Cutlets, with Peas, 85
—— ——, Cucumbers, 86
Lard, how to, 15
Larded Sweetbreads, 107
Lemon Blancmange, 178
—— Custard Puddings, 175
—— Jelly, 173
—— Pudding, 189
Lobster Butter, 164
—— Salad, 160
—— Sauce, 60
—— Stewed, 158
—— Vol au vent, 86
Loin of Mutton, boned, 129

MACARONI and Cheese, 155
—— Timbales, 100
Mackerel, Maître d'Hôtel Sauce, 67
—— Fillets of, 66
Mayonnaise Sauce, 159
Meat Jelly, 160
Melted Butter, 53
—— —— French, 162
Mushroom Sauce, 134
Mustard Sauce, 67
Mutton Broth, 45

INDEX.

Mutton Cutlets, with Fried Potatoes, 76
———— Sauce Italienne, 77
———— aux Coucombres, 77
———— à la Maintenon, 78
———— à la Reforme, 78
———— à la Soubise, 79
———— aux Marrons, 80
———— Haricot, 81
———— Loin of, 129
———— Saddle of, 129

NORMANDY Pippins, 187

OMELETTE, Remarks on Making, 151
———— aux fines Herbes, 151
———— Cheese, 152
———— Ham, 152
———— Kidneys, 152
———— Sweet, 191
Onion Soup, 46
Orange Jelly, 173
———— Compôte of, 188
Oysters, Vol au Vent of, 87
———— in Shells, 155
Oyster Sauce, 56
———— Toast, 156

PEA Soup, 45
Peas, 122
———— Purée of Green, 122
———— Preserved Green, 123
Parsley Sauce, 55
Partridge, 145
Pheasant, Boiled, 146
———— Salmi of, 106
Pigeons, 109
Piquante Sauce, 84
Poivrade Sauce, 84
Pot au Feu, 33
Potage Printanier, 39

Potatoes, Maître d'Hotel Sauce, 115
———— Purée of, 116
———— Sieved, 115
———— Soufflés, 116
Prawn Salad, 160
———— Stewed, 158
Pudding, Adelaide, 179
———— Alexandra, 190
———— Albert, 177
———— Bordeaux, 182
———— Bread and Butter, 176
———— Grape, 182
———— Clara, 180
———— Madelaine, 181
———— Victoria, 180
———— Plum, 178
———— Rice, 177
———— Tapioca, 176
———— Madame Angôt, 181
———— German Cabinet, 190
———— Diplomate, 179

QUENELLES of Rabbit, 92

RICE à l'Imperatrice, 169
———— for Curry, 95
———— Pudding, 177
———— Soup, 35
Reine, Soup à la, 46
Rabbit, Quenelles of, 92
———— Cutlets, 105
———— Soup, 43
Rolled Loin of Mutton, 129
Roast Chickens, 136
———— Lamb, 133
———— Turkey, 136
———— Goose, 137
———— Woodcock, 144
———— Grouse, 145
———— Partridge, 145
———— Guinea Fowl, 143
———— Ducks, 137
———— Wild Duck, 145

INDEX.

Roast Snipe, 145

SAUCE à la Tartare, 93
—— Anchovy, 57
—————— (rich), 57
—— Apple and Chestnut, 138
—— Béarnise, 63
—— Bread, 137
—— Butter (melted), 53
—— Celery, 135
—— Chestnut, 138
—— Cream, 146
—— Dutch, 58
—— Groseille, 105
—— Guards, 183
—— Horse Radish (iced), 63
—— Impèratrice, 54
—— Italienne, 77
—— Lobster, 60
—— Mayonnaise, 159
—— Mustard, 67
—— Mushroom, 134
—— Oyster, 56
—— Parsley, 55
—— Piquante, 84
—— Poivrade, 84
—— for Puddings, 175
—— Salad, 159
—— Shrimp, 55
—— Soubise, 80
—— Tarragon, 135
—— Tomato, 65
—— Thickening for, 82
—— Truffle, 91
—— White, 85, 134
—— Wine, 175
Salsifis, 119
—— Scalloped, 120
Saddle of Mutton, 129
—— of Lamb, 133
Salad, Lobster, 160
—— Prawn, 160
—— Sauce, 159
—— Winter, 160

Salmi, Pheasant, 106
—— Wild Duck, 106
Salmon, 62
—— Rissoles, 63
Scolloped Eggs, 155
Scollops, Beef, 88
—— Veal, 102
Scotch Woodcock, 153
Sardines with Oil, 164
Shoulder of Lamb, 133
Semolina Blancmange, 184
Seville Orange Biscuits, 196
Skate, au Beurre Noir, 68
Soles, Boiled, 53
—— au Vin Blanc, 64
—— Boiled Fillets of, 64
—— Fillets of, à la Horly, 64
—— ————, and Anchovies, 66
Sorrel, Purèe of, 132
—— with Eggs, 120
Soubise Sauce, 80
Souche Water, 68
Soufflé, 170
—— Cheese, 153
—— Coffee, 171
—— Chocolate, 171
—— Cream, 171
—— Fruits, 182
Soups, to clear, 32
Spinach, 117
Stewed Lobster, 158
—— Prawns, 158
—— Peaches, 188
—— Sirloin of Beef, 131
Straws, Cheese, 157
Swiss Cream, 187
—— Soup, 41
Sweetbreads, 107
—— Lambs, in Scollops, 85

TAPIOCA Soup, 34
—— Pudding, 176
Tarragon Sauce, 135
Toasted Cheese, 157

Tomato Sauce, 65
Thick Oxtail Soup, 44
Timbales, Bread, 174
—— Macaroni, 100
Truffle Sauce, 91
Turnips with Cream, 117
Turbot, 59
—— au Gratin, 61
Turkey, Roast, with Oysters, 136
—— Boiled, 134
—— Poults, 143
Turtle Soup, 36

VANILLE Sugar, 169
Vermicelli Soup, 34
Veal Scollops, 102

Veal Cutlets, German, 101
—— —— à la Bourgeoise, 131
Victoria Pudding, 180
Vol au Vent, Lobster, 86
—— Shrimps, 86
—— Prawns, 86
—— Oyster, 87
—— à la Béchamel, 87

WATER Souché, 68
White Sauce, 85, 134
—— Stock, 31
Wild Duck, 145
Winter Salad, 160
Woodcock, 144
—— Scotch, 153

NEW BOOKS RECENTLY PUBLISHED

BY

KERBY & ENDEAN,

THE HISTORY OF COACHES.

By G. A. THRUPP. Demy 8vo, beautifully illustrated, cloth, 6s.

"Mr Thrupp has very successfully narrated the history of coaches from a coach builder's point of view. But people who want to be able to distinguish between berlins, landaus, curricles, tilburies, broughams, phaetons, briskas, stanhopes, and many more, and to know why they were called by such names, will find full information here. There are many pictures of all kinds, ranging from an Egyptian chariot to a modern French diligence, and the text is much elucidated by them."—*Saturday Review.*

"The volume is specially interesting to coach-builders, to antiquaries, and to anyone who wishes to know how the world has moved in the last four or five thousand years."—*Glasgow Herald.*

"Is an important volume, an almost exhaustive book of reference on the subject of coaches."—*Christian World.*

"Contains much curious and interesting matter about vehicles of various kinds in all ages and almost all countries, and it is put into a very popular shape." —*City Press.*

"A survey at once historical and artistic of carriages and carriage-building, from the dawn of history till now, . . . a volume for the coach-builder in the first instance, is rich in rare antiquarian details, set off by curious illustrations--a book of equal interest to the lover of old fashions, or the practical student of modern industries."—*Graphic.*

"The coaching renaissance of the last few years would not have been complete without the issue of a work dealing with coaches in all ages, and so here we have it at last, an authentic history of the various traps in which man has driven since he first learned the noble art of coachmanship."—*Globe.*

"Readers wishing for general or special informaiton with regard to the art of coach-building will do well to consult these pages."—*Pall Mall Gazette.*

LAPLAND LIFE:

Or Summer Adventures in the Arctic Regions. By the Reverend DONALD D. MACKINNON, M.A., beautifully illustrated from original designs. Crown 8vo, cloth, 5s.

New Books Recently Published by

FROM CALAIS TO KARLSBAD.

By T. LOUIS OXLEY. Crown 8vo, cloth, illustrated, 5s.

THE SIGNATURE OF GUTHENBERG.

By P. DE VILLIERS, M.D., royal 8vo, with copies of the Signature and of the Indulgence on the back of which the Signature was written. *A very remarkable discovery in connexion with the Inventor of Printing.*

LAS MEMORIAS AND VERS DE SOCIETE.

By A. F. A. W. Crown 8vo, 2 vols., cloth, 10s.

LENDING UNTO THE LORD;

Or, Three Days in the Life of Christian Fürchtegott Gellert, Poet and Professor in Leipsic University. By BARON CONWAY and J. RUSSELL ENDEAN. Illustrated from original designs by the Hon. CHARLOTTE ELLIS. Royal 16mo, 3s.

"I hope 'Lending unto the Lord' will have the good effect of recommending the duty of Christian benevolence which it inculcates."—*His Grace the Archbishop of Canterbury.*

"An important work, which the Archbishop hopes to read with the attention which it deserves."—*His Grace the Archbishop of York.*

"Dear Sir,—I thank you much for sending me a copy of your beautiful little work, 'Lending Unto the Lord.' It is fitted to encourage such lending as, I fear, is too rare, and, independently of this, to interest and please thoughtful Christian minds and hearts. Very truly yours, John Cumming. To J. Russell Endean, Esq."—*Rev. John Cumming, D.D., F.R.S.E.*

"It is a delightful little book."—*Rev. Donald Fraser, D.D.*

"'Lending unto the Lord' is an interesting book. It is nicely written, and ought to prove popular in the circle of readers to whom it is addressed."—*Athenæum.*

"This is a very pretty gift-book. It relates an event in the life of Gellert, the hymn-writer of Leipsic, in which his lending to the Lord met with a rich reward."—*The English Churchman.*

"'Lending Unto the Lord' came safely, and I read it through with much interest. I have written a notice for 'Sword and Trowel.'"—*Rev. C. H. Spurgeon.*

"'Lending Unto the Lord' is a good book. The story brought the water into our eyes as we read it. It ought to sell by thousands. The narrative is calculated to foster that spirit of benevolence which is the glory of Christianity."—*Sword and Trowel.*

"Is a religious narration of an admirable and earnest Christian. Prefixed is a remarkable and pretty hymn, by Julia B. Endean, at the age of 12. The volume would make a pretty Sunday present."—*Publisher's Circular.*

"This is an excellent little book. The incidents are deeply interesting, and convey an excellent moral."—*Court Journal.*

"A charming picture of a portion of a happy, benevolent Christian life."—*Evening Standard.*

"This is a very delightful story, both as to its subject and the manner of telling. It is true, and will find interested readers among old as well as young We can heartily commend the book on every account."—*Church Bells.*

"This is a most interesting tale, excellently-well and naturally rendered. It includes a poem, written by Miss J. Beatall Endean, at the age of 12 years, remarkable for the psychological culture it reveals, and for command of the forms of verse."—*Bayswater Chronicle.*

JOAN OF ARC:

A Poem. By ROBERT BLAKE. Crown 8vo, toned, cloth, 3s. 6d.

"The verse is harmonious, flowing and easy. The poem does honour to its author."—*Siècle.*

"Very beautiful and highly poetical."—*Poet's Magazine.*

SACRED LYRICS.

By HENRY LOCKWOOD, Author of "Axel and other Poems." Super-royal 16mo, toned, cloth, 4s. 6d.

THE MARIA STIEG, AND OTHER POEMS.

By FRANCES JANE FORSAYTH, Authoress of "Amos Waters and other Poems." 12mo, cloth, 3s. 6d.

DAILY DEVOTION :

Or, Prayers Framed on the Successive Portions of the New Testament as Appointed in the New Lectionary, to which are added Forms of Prayer for a Fortnight, for Family or Private Use. By DANIEL MOORE, M.A., Chaplain in Ordinary to the Queen, and Vicar of Holy Trinity, Paddington. Large crown 8vo, cloth, 6s.

"This book provides a prayer suitable for family worship for every morning and evening of the year, and there is added a Form for Family Devotion for a Fortnight."—*English Churchman.*

"An excellent compilation. This useful Manual of Daily Devotion is admirably adapted for family or private use."—*Court Journal.*

"The book will be very useful for reading aloud, or for family prayers."—*The Bookseller.*

"'Daily Devotion' consists of excellent Scripture prayers for day-by-day service, and some occasional prayers. They are well written, and we can strongly commend them as suitable to all families."—*Publishers' Circular.*

"A valuable aid to devotion, and the publishers have displayed much taste and care in its appearance."—*Western Daily Mercury.*

CHRISTIAN CONSOLATION:

Or, Discourses on the Reliefs afforded by the Gospel under different States and Trials of the Christian Life. By DANIEL MOORE, M.A., Chaplain in Ordinary to the Queen, and Vicar of Holy Trinity, Paddington. 12mo, cloth, 5s.

DISCOURSES ON THE LORD'S PRAYER.

By the Rev. DANIEL MOORE, M.A., Chaplain in Ordinary to the Queen, and Vicar of Holy Trinity, Paddington. 12mo, cloth, 5s.

PRIVATE DEVOTIONS FOR GIRLS.

With Maxims and Rules of Conduct at Home and at School; with Suggestions for a Young Lady's English Education. Royal 32mo, cloth, 6d.

"Plain, simple, and yet thoroughly well written, this book for the use of young ladies may be put into their hands by parents with the fullest confidence. Heads of schools will find it a great help in the government of their pupils."

CHRISTIAN TOLERATION:

An Essay. By the Honourable A. S. G. CANNING. Large crown 8vo, toned, 3s. 6d.

"Everybody should read the Honourable A. S. G. Canning's Original Essay on Christian Toleration."

ANONYMOUS CRITICISM:

An Essay. By ROBERT BLAKE. Demy 8vo, 1s.

"There are few ideas in this Essay with which we do not thoroughly agree."—*Cambridge Express.*

"The style is terse and perspicuous, graceful, yet trenchant. The phraseology is at times very beautiful."—*Tyrone Constitution.*

BEING IN THE CHOIR:

An Address to Church Singers on their Duties and Responsibilities. By a Clergyman. New edition, revised, 12mo, tinted wrapper, 3d.; or per dozen, 2s. 6d.

LIFE MARINERS:

Or, Homeward Bound. By BOUCHIER PHILLIMORE. Royal 16mo, cloth, 1s.

ENDEAN'S GAME BOOK.

Imperial 8vo, oblong, 10s. 6d. Tabulated and appropriately illustrated by the Honourable CHARLOTTE ELLIS. This is a book that should be in use by every Sportsman, as it is provided for the purpose of recording the results of sport from one end of the year to the other, with the Hounds, Rod, or Gun.

THE HISTORY OF THREE LITTLE PIGS.

Beautifully illustrated from original designs by the Hon. CHARLOTTE ELLIS. Imperial 8vo, printed in photo-lithography, 3s. 6d. A charming book for a child.

THE BLUE RIBBONS:

A Story of the Last Century. By ANNA HARRIET DRURY, Authoress of "Deep Waters," "Misrepresentation," &c. Illustrated by Birket Foster. Square 12mo, cloth, 3s. 6d.

HAPPY HOURS:

Or, the Home Story Book. By MARY CHERWELL. With illustrations from designs by Sir John Gilbert. Square cloth, 2s. 6d.

THE DIETETICS OF THE SOUL;

Or, True Mental Discipline. By ERNEST FEUCHTERSLEBEN, M.D.. Translated from the 32d German edition by Colonel OUVRY, C.B. Fcap. 8vo, cloth, 2s. 6d.

"This is a consideration of the conditions under which the mind and spirit can be kept in health. It is written with a pure tone, and opposed to material tendencies."—*Nonconformist.*

"It contains many excellent suggestions."—*Christian World.*

"The leading thought is the intimate connection between bodily and spiritual health."—*Saturday Review.*

STEIN, AND HIS REFORMS IN PRUSSIA.

With Reference to the Land Question in England. By Col. H. A. OUVRY, C.B. Crown 8vo, cloth, 2s. 6d.

"Every one should read and digest every word in this book. In one short paragraph of Col. Ouvry's we have stated the absolute necessity of restoring the peasantry to the land, the violence that of old drove them from the soil, the necessity of many peasant proprietors to give strength and stability to the institutions of the country; that peasant proprietorship improves the character as well as the condition of the people; and lastly, when the masses depend wholly on precarious wages, they are dangerous to the State, and have too little respect for the rights of property."—*Labourer's Union Chronicle.*

"A really valuable work: it ought to be in the hands of all who are interested in the Land Question."—*Nonconformist.*

ODD SHOWERS;

Or, an Explanation of the Rain of Insects, Fishes, and Lizards; Soot, Sand and Ashes; Red Rain and Snow; Meteoric Stones and other Bodies. By CARRIBER. Square 16mo, 1s.

TO AUTHORS.

How to Publish, and on the Easiest Terms.

MESSRS KERBY & ENDEAN'S large experience in the trade and personal practical knowledge of everything connected with the production of books, from the setting of the first types to the placing of the complete book in the hands of the public, are a sufficient guarantee that all that can be done to render books successful will be done by them, and they place their services at the command of authors about to publish. They undertake commissions for every class of publication,—religious, scientific, political, educational, &c. Sermons and pamphlets produced at the shortest notice, and in the best style.

www.ingramcontent.com/pod-product-compliance
Lightning Source LLC
Chambersburg PA
CBHW020902230426
43666CB00008B/1286